D1740848

ENOUGH WITH THE BULL

A JOURNAL FOR YOUNG ADULTS ABOUT RELATIONSHIPS AND CONSENT

NICOLE CAMPBELL

WAYS TO USE THIS JOURNAL

Well, in all reality, you could use it however you want, but I figured at least a layout would be helpful.

This book contains six sections, and they are meant to go in order because each builds on the work done in the previous section. In each one, you'll find an introduction, at least one short story with discussion questions, and a journal for you to sort through your own thoughts. That being said, if you skip around, no one will come to yell at you.

This journal has a companion parent journal as well, but it can absolutely be used alone, so if that's you, no worries.

If you currently have a partner, significant other, friend with benefits... anyone you consider yourself having a relation-ship with, it would be really beneficial for you to work through the journal at the same time and have some really in-depth discussions. If you're currently thinking "I could never do that and talk about these types of thoughts with him/her/them," then I say to you, *challenge accepted*. The whole point of this book is to lessen the general awkwardness of having these conversations. So, I hope by the end, you feel differently if that was your initial reaction.

Also, please write in the journal. Not necessarily to share with anyone, but to hold yourself accountable to your own thoughts. It's a lot harder to backtrack when it's in writing.

Other than that, welcome, thank you for picking up this journal, even if your parents or guardians made you do it. I think you'll learn something about yourself by the end.

FOREWORD AND DEDICATION

At the beginnings of the #MeToo movement, and really well before that, I knew I needed to write this collection. Beyond these stories, I also knew that I needed to do what I do best, which is teach, and that is where the journal part of this collection fits in.

I cannot claim to have all of the answers or to possess the ability to "fix" the very serious problems we have in our society surrounding the issues of consent. I also cannot single-handedly address the absence of comprehensive sex education that should include how to build, participate in, and demand healthy relationships. There are some things, however, that I've learned along the way that I know can change individual experiences—and that matters.

If you've picked up this book, whether it be for yourself, your child, or even to make sense out of your own experiences, know that it is dedicated to you. I wrote it for myself, I wrote it for the students I have spent my career worrying about and learning from, and for everyone who is with me in wanting to make a change in the statistics that tell us things are definitely not all right.

The title for this collection came about because I got so tired of hearing these old clichés about how girls or boys are supposed to act. I realized that expectations for young people are really set *so low*, and that's a problem. I've worked with teenagers for most of my career, and this idea that you all can't figure things out or make good decisions is just false. When given sound information and room to think it through, I've seen exactly the opposite.

So yes, I will spend the rest of my time here in the next hundred pages or so dispelling the myth that anything in the human experience of relationships is black and white or able to fit into a neat little box. This book is not here to warn you or judge you or scare you. It is here to make you think about your own life and boundaries and to make decisions based on what's best for you.

<3 Nicole

FIGURING IT OUT

Why buy the cow when you can get the milk for free?

— AMERICAN IDIOM

This old saying is problematic for several reasons. One, it compares people to cows, and is therefore off to a poor start. Two, it assumes that this cow-buying person is only interested in milk and nothing else. I would keep this metaphor going, but it's disturbing, really. I've found that people like simplistic ideas that cover a wide variety of scenarios, and this is one of them. Except it doesn't even begin to dive into the complexity of human emotions and relationships. So, forget the cow, and worry about the farm as a whole. Yeah, no, that analogy still isn't working for me.

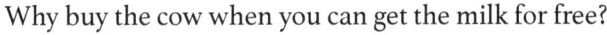

There is no shortage of YA (Young Adult) stories out there that deal with young people "figuring out" relationships. My issue with this is that I don't see enough of real life reflected in mainstream YA contemporary literature, especially when the truth is uncomfortable. That being said, I absolutely applaud and support authors who are making a point to change things.

This section, to me, means dealing with the sort of stories that almost everyone can relate to. The stories that show us the general awkwardness and sometimes very real fear of figuring out how to tell people how we feel, risk rejection, decide how we feel versus how we're supposed to feel, and more. There's no roadmap for this, because everyone has different boundaries, different life experiences, different fears, and different desires. There's no one way to approach communicating with someone you have (or want to have) a relationship with.

There are some pretty clear lines, however, on how *not* to communicate—rage, manipulation, verbal or physical abuse. Unfortunately, these reactions seem almost commonplace when some people face rejection. Really, what that looks like to an outside observer is the lack of a coping strategy for dealing with hurt and rejection, along with a lack of resilience.

I hope that you'll consider the motivations behind each of these characters' actions and envision yourself in similar situations. Here's to all of us who are figuring it out.

<3 Nicole

A LIONESS, A WITCH, AND AN ISSUE WITH THE WARDROBE

It was one of those days when I thought I might actually do it. I might tell Rowyn that I couldn't be her best friend. I couldn't just be the guy who listened to all of the girl talk. I had to have something more, or I had to just get some damn distance from her.

"Reed. Why do you have that look on your face?" Rose asked while we walked down the hall to bio. I hated the first day back after winter break. It was like time moved in slow motion, and I didn't know of any reliable spell-work to speed up time.

"Would it be completely stupid for me to give Rowyn, like, an ultimatum?" My hands found their way through my black wavy hair, knowing the answer already.

"You want to give her an ultimatum before you've even told her you have all sorts of loving, lustful feelings for her?" Rose's tone didn't change... just her side-eye.

"You want me to believe that she doesn't know exactly how I feel about her?"

3

"I don't... I don't know."

"All right, spill it. Whatever it is. You *always* know."

"I hate it when you guys do this to me." Rose flipped her long blond hair, and that let me know she was getting ready to tell me anyway, even though she didn't want to. There were some advantages to knowing someone your entire life.

"I have no idea what you're talking about."

"I can't keep a secret for one of you without being a shitty friend to the other, and you know it." My stomach dropped when I felt the shift in her energy hit me. All I felt was deceit. Instead of finishing the walk to class, I pulled Rose into the media center.

"Yeah, you're going to have to go ahead and explain, because your anxiety is throwing me." I didn't usually have to shield myself around Rose; she was too steady, and too freaking happy all the time for it to bother me.

"Whatever. There was a thing at Yule with that guy Ryan, and-"

"What did he do?"

"Oh my god, nothing. I mean, nothing you need to pull out your boxing skills for."

"Then what?"

"They just... I think she likes him? And some things may have gone on? I don't know."

She was lying again, but I let it go this time because I didn't know if I could take knowing what "things" were. "At Yule?"

She bit her lip. "Yeah."

"And you said *nothing* to me for two weeks?"

"Reed. I —it's not always so simple with the two of you."

"Got it. Thanks." I pushed back open the door to the hallway and didn't care in the slightest that I'd be late. It also gave me a petty sense of satisfaction that Rose would too, and I knew how much it bothered her not to be punctual. I slid into my chair and let the glare from Mr. Wills roll off of me.

Rowyn had spent all of Yule sitting on my lap. Her hair had smelled like winter, and when she played with the rings on my fingers in front of the fire, it made my chest hurt in a way that I couldn't stop through any means of energy work. She hadn't pulled away when I held her hand, or even when I pressed my lips to the back of her neck. I vaguely remembered watching Rose and Rowyn leave the house— they looked like light and dark in balance when they were together. Rose and her white-blond hair and unfailing positive outlook, and Rowyn with her black curls and an attitude that rightfully frightened most other humans.

But none of it meant anything to her. I'd met Ryan a couple of times at Full Moon or Litha—some of the bigger holidays we celebrated. And I almost laughed out loud because there was no way that a guy like Ryan Summerton could even come close to handling Rowyn's particular brand of crazy. But it still hurt that she... whatever she did.

It was clear that if I had any sense of self-preservation, I should just make the choice and get some distance. I couldn't deal with sitting by and watching her date someone else. It would kill me. *Maybe it will be enough to get over her.*

I hauled ass to my Jetta after the last bell. It was one hundred percent passive-aggressive, because I usually gave Row a ride home, but I didn't know what would come out of my mouth if I sat alone in the car with her. I went to open my driver's side door, and I noticed a very angry blond standing in front of the Jeep parked next to me, kicking a very flat tire and yelling at her cell phone.

"Uh, do you need some help?"

"*No, I'm perfectly*—" She looked up and stopped talking. I knew her. Our town had three thousand people in it; I knew everyone. And there was no doubt she knew me. Her dad was one of the pastors in town, and he wasn't a real big fan of the neighborhood witches. She cleared her throat, and her energy went from angry to open in the blink of an eye. I sometimes had that effect on people. They liked to vent to me. "I—well. This tire is flat, my brother and dad aren't answering their phones, and I have no idea how to fix it."

Half of me just wanted to get out of there before Rowyn got to the car and saw me talking to Amy Stecker and had a stroke. There was no love lost between the two of them. The other half of me felt like I needed to help her and that the whole situation was doing a decent job of taking my mind off of everything else. "Do you have a spare?"

"I think this was the spare," she said, referencing the flat tire and biting her lip.

I laughed. I couldn't help it.

And then she went back to glaring at me. "You don't have to help me. I'm certain someone more capable of—"

"Slow your roll, Amy. I'm sorry I laughed. Get in the car, we'll go get a tire, and I'll bring you back and put it on for you."

"You aren't going to try to kidnap me, are you?"

"I'm sorry, I'm having a hard time determining when you're being serious. Everything that comes out of your mouth is just sort of—"

"Okay, shut up. I'll get in the car." And she did, throwing her purse sort of violently in the back seat while she was at it. "So, where are we going?"

"My brother works at the shop on Main. We'll go there."

"Are you really this nice of a person?"

"Nice enough to drive you to get a tire? Yeah, it looks that way. Is that a personality trait you look for in a man?" I had to at least goad her a little bit after the kidnapping comment.

"I don't see any men around here, otherwise I'd tell you."

"That's the best you've got? You're Amy Stecker. You're supposed to hit me with some serious pride-wounding shit here. I'm disappointed." She started laughing then. It was kind of a nice sound. She was one of those girls who had a perma-frown and complained a lot. People just let her get away with it because she was a Stecker. And she was hot. It had to be said.

"Maybe I am off my game a bit."

"Everything okay?" I didn't even know why I asked. We weren't friends by any means, but I could feel the information at the edge of her consciousness.

"No, not really. My dad wants to send me to a religious school in Bethel. With only girls."

"Why? Isn't he big on supporting the community and whatnot?"

"Because he walked in on me making out with Kyle."

"Oh. Well, I guess that would do it."

Kyle was the wide receiver of Constitution High's football team. He was also one of the only black kids at our high school. I wished that wasn't where my mind went immediately, but, well, that's where it went.

"Right. Because Bobby's never felt some girl up on our couch before. It's such a double standard I can't even take it."

Bobby Stecker was Amy's older brother. For him? I would not have offered to help with the tire. The word *sociopath* usually came up in conversations about Bobby. Amy started messing with the buttons on my stereo, and I had to fight the urge to treat her like I would Rose or Rowyn and smack her hand away from my music.

"I didn't really think of that. I only have the one brother. But yeah, that sucks. Does your mom want you to go too?"

"Whatever Daddy says, my mother says too. It's like living in an episode of Leave It to Beaver."

"Your pop culture references surprise me, Amy." I pulled into the tiny parking lot at the body shop where my brother Cole worked. The expression on his face when he saw who I was with absolutely readable as shock, but to his

8

credit, he acted like the whole situation was normal and got the girl the right tire.

"It should only take a minute when we're back to school to get it changed."

"Well, in that case, do you wanna stop and get candy?"

"You want to stop and get candy."

"Yeah, that's what I said. At the Candy Striper Shop."

"Um, sure?"

"Well, you helped me with this stupid tire, and you were actually surprisingly nice, so I figured I could buy you some gumdrops or something. Whatever. We don't have to go."

She was *nervous*. And I was loving it a little bit.

"First of all? No one in their right mind likes *gumdrops*. But you can buy me some candy. And if you want, I'll even share it with you." I grinned at her eye roll, but drove to the candy shop anyway.

———

"Why do you only like sour candy?"

"Because it's the best kind of candy. Everyone knows that. There are so many things I could teach you. How to change a tire, appropriate candy selection. We should have been friends a long time ago, and you might not be in this predicament today."

"We're not... are we friends?"

"I don't know, Amy. I helped a damsel in distress and now she's going to feed me. It seems like we are, at the very least, friends."

"You're kind of weird."

"I get that a lot."

"I think I like it, though."

"I get that a lot, too." She smacked my arm and paid for our brown paper sack of candy.

"Let's go to the park and eat it before we go back to school," she commanded.

"Amy, I don't mean to alarm you, but to some people it would look like you're trying to spend more time with me. On purpose."

"Really? I would think that to some people it would look like you were trying to kidnap me. Weird." She shrugged, and I realized she was a lot different that I'd assumed.

"Definitely weird."

———

I was sitting in my car, eating candy with Amy Stecker, idling at the park. And it wasn't even that awkward. I also appreciated that I hadn't had the opportunity to dissect the Rowyn situation.

"So, are you going to kiss me?" Amy asked plainly, and I almost choked on my sour patch kid. There was a very solid line between mildly flirting with a girl like her and making a move on a girl like her.

"Do you *want* me to kiss you?"

"If you want to." *Yeah, no.*

"Sorry, I don't really play that game." The afternoon had gotten away from me, so I moved to put the car in reverse to head back to school.

"Fine, Jesus. I want you to kiss me. So could you just?"

I looked up, really wondering what the hell the universe was trying to do to me today, but there was no reason I couldn't kiss Amy. Rowyn wasn't mine, and I didn't know that she'd ever be. I breathed out to diffuse the awkwardness of it all, but leaned over the gearshift and pressed my lips to hers lightly. She invited me in, and within moments, the mood was much more serious. She climbed over the console to sit on my lap and I ran my thumb along her jaw.

Fifteen minutes later, Amy had taken off her sweater and was working on the button to my pants, but her energy was wrong. It was angry.

"Amy..." I got out while she moved her mouth to my neck. Being an empath absolutely *sucked* sometimes, but I wasn't okay with doing anything if she was only doing it to get back at her dad.

"Reed..." she answered.

"Just, ah, are you okay?"

"Um, what?"

"Are you okay? You seem angry, which is kind of... I don't know. Just, are you okay?"

"Yes, Reed, I'm just great. I'm half-naked in your car on our first non-date, and now you think I'm a slut."

"No no no no no. That's not... no. I... well, I read energy. And you just feel... angry. I know that sounds weird, I just don't know how else to explain it. And I don't wanna do something that you'll regret when you're not angry anymore."

"I wonder what that would be like," she let out, moving back to her own seat.

"I'm sorry, I didn't mean to-"

"Just take me back to my car."

"Okay."

———

It was a quiet ride back to school.

"I swear to God, Reed Hansen, if you tell anyone about this, I will—"

"Hey, can I just be real with you for a second?"

"I guess I don't really have a choice, since I can't leave until you fix my car."

"Yeah, no. You always have a choice. I don't know what kind of guys you've dated, but I will absolutely change your tire and leave you alone if that's what you want. I just... I think you've got me wrong."

She sat quietly, but she didn't move to get out of the car.

"I had actual *fun* this afternoon, on what was trying to be a really terrible day. And I was totally into what we were doing at the park… I just felt like something was off, and I can't really just turn it off, what I do with reading energy. And I didn't want to. I needed to know if you were into it too. So don't be worried about me, like, talking shit or whatever. I'm big on karma, so, I can change your tire, and we can pretend this never happened, or we could do candy at the park again another day. Or dinner. Or something."

"You're going to think I'm a horrible person if I tell you what I'm thinking.

"Maybe." She glared at me at that.

"I had fun today too, but my dad would absolutely flip if I went on a date with you. Like… his health would actually be in danger."

"Yeah. I could see that."

"But I would like to eat candy at the park with you again."

"So you just want to secretly make out and eat candy."

"Well, the candy wouldn't have to be a secret. But the other… yeah."

Maybe I was the horrible person, because that sounded like exactly what I needed. I leaned over and kissed her again.

Read more about Reed and Amy in Nicole Campbell's full-length novel,
The Tower

Why is Reed so afraid to tell Rowyn how he feels if they've been friends for years? Are his fears justified? What is the best-case and worst-case scenario if he had that conversation with her?

_____

_____

_____

_____

_____

What are Reed's motives for kissing Amy? How do those compare with Amy's motives for kissing Reed? What is your opinion about their situation?

_____

_____

_____

_____

_____

How did Reed diffuse the tension with Amy after he stopped them from going any further in the car? How did he make her understand that he wasn't rejecting her, and why do you think she jumped to that conclusion in the first place?

_____

_____

_____

_____

_____

Just based on this story, how do you think Rowyn might react to Reed's secret with Amy?

_____

_____

_____

_____

_____

What can you take away from this story?

_____

_____

_____

_____

_____

.   .   .

Thoughts:

_____

_____

_____

_____

_____

_____

_____

_____

_____

_____

_____

_____

_____

_____

TRUTH, TRUST, AND TIMING

Tears stung my eyes as I let myself out the front door of Luke's house. I knew I was being a dick when I'd said it, but it wasn't until Vanessa lost her damn mind that I realized just how badly I'd screwed up.

"Do you ever think about Zack Roads when you and Luke are getting it on? Like a flash of his dreamy blue eyes just appears in your mind when-" Luke was up off of the floor before I could finish the next word, but Vanessa was faster. She was straddling my lap in a way that made me cringe, but the look on her face was pure fury.

"You wanna hear all about Zack Roads, Troy?" She was practically touching my nose with hers, and I wanted to push her away.

"I was just messing around, Jesus. You are insane." My eyes darted around quickly, looking for an ally, but there was nothing but support for V in that room.

"Yep, that's me. Totally insane that I would be offended when you bring up the guy who punched me in the face last year after

calling me a whore. I'm so *crazy because I don't think you're hilarious for bringing him up, knowing that Luke had to beat the shit out of him to get him off of me in the parking lot. Maybe I'm not insane. Maybe you're just a fucking dick, Troy. Get bent.*"

Maybe you are *just a dick*, I thought to myself. I'd known things hadn't ended well with Vanessa and Zack, but I never thought he'd *hurt* her. I just wanted... I wanted her to disappear. *So that what? You can have your shot with Luke?* I felt more tears on my face. I swung open my car door and fell into the driver's seat, wishing I could take back the entire night.

There was absolutely no reason I should have agreed to hang out. It was hard enough watching him with her at school, knowing there was *nothing* I could do to change things. But seeing them together tonight was too much. Every time Luke grabbed my shoulder or brushed my hand while passing me a beer, it made my brain want to explode.

And he just kicked you out of his house. I hadn't meant for it to go that far, to piss either of them off that much. I'd just wanted to... make them both feel as crappy as I felt. *Yep, you're a dick.* I started the car once my eyes cleared, wishing I knew how I was going to fix this.

———

The lights were on in the kitchen when I pulled into my driveway. *Shit.* I really just wanted to get to my room and not deal with anyone else. I slipped in through the front door, and my mom appeared out of thin air.

"You're home early for a Saturday." Her eyes looked worried, and I hated it.

"Yeah. I was tired." I desperately tried to hide the thickness in my voice from crying.

"Troy…"

"Mom, I'm fine, seriously." She looked me over carefully, and I knew she was debating how far she wanted to push the issue.

"Okay… but if you need anything…"

"Got it," I breathed out and trudged up the stairs to my room. I'd come out to my mom six months before, but she was the only one in my family who knew. Telling her had been hard enough. I knew she wanted to be supportive, but she always looked at me a little like I was an alien and she didn't know what language I spoke.

I flopped onto my bed, wishing I could fall asleep, but knowing I couldn't, and took out my phone. I typed too many texts and deleted each and every one. I didn't know how to explain to Luke without *explaining* to Luke. Another part of me just wanted to get it over with. Tell him I was in love with him and transfer schools or fall in a hole or something. I didn't know how to move on and pretend just to be his friend, and it was killing me.

There was nothing I could type that was sufficient, so I decided to stare at the ceiling instead and worry about it tomorrow.

———

I sat on his porch for a good forty-five minutes the following evening after he hadn't answered my calls all day.

"Troy, man, what do you want?" Luke called when he stepped out of his truck. I stood and shoved my hands in my jean pockets.

"I guess to apologize."

"I'm not really the one who needs it. So lemme know how your conversation with Vanessa goes." Luke walked past me and into the house, though he left the door open behind him. I shuffled in after.

"Yeah. I'll call her. Or maybe I'll text her. I didn't know that shit about Roads. I wouldn't have... I don't know, I know I'm a dick to her, but I wouldn't have said *that*."

"Normally, I'd call you out for being afraid of her, but she was in rare form tonight, so maybe texting would be a better idea. And you know you don't actually *have to* be a dick to her. Unless you, like, wrote it down in your diary or took a sacred oath or something. You could just keep your mouth shut." Luke took down a shot glass and grabbed a bottle of vodka. "Do you want one?" he asked me after he took the first.

"What's going on with you, anyway?" I didn't answer about the shot, so Luke took another. Something was off.

"Nothing, man. Just another fun-filled Saturday night."

"If she makes you this crazy... why do you deal with her?" I knew I was dangerously close to saying something I couldn't take back.

"You think I'm drinking because my girlfriend is crazy? If that were the case, I'd have a much bigger problem."

I took down my own shot glass and toyed with it, spinning it on the counter. "Okay, then. Whatever you say."

"Don't act like you fucking know what my life is like, T." The words stung when they landed.

"Like you're the only one with shit going on, Luke? Everybody has their own stuff to deal with." My voice nearly broke just at that, and I had no idea how I'd ever be able to tell him the truth. But I also couldn't stand the look of hurt on his face.

"Yeah? Well, at least you get to deal with yours in your house, where people give a damn about what happens to you." He took another shot.

"What are you talking about? What's going on with your mom?"

"She's just campaigning for parent of the year again."

"By..."

"Spending the entire college fund that my grandma left me, getting fired for drinking at work, not paying bills... I could make you a list."

"Shit." I let out a breath. "I'm sorry."

"Don't be. Not your problem. I'll be my uncle's problem now, I guess."

"Wait... you're *leaving*?" All of the air was being sucked out of my lungs.

"That I am."

"Like school, and everything?" I knew it was hard to see him and not have him see me the same way, but I didn't know if I could deal with not seeing him at all.

"No. I don't know. I don't know anything anymore. Just go home. Call Vanessa." Luke downed another shot and was apparently done talking.

"If there's anything I can-"

"Just *go*, T."

So I did. I could hear the blood rushing in my ears, and my heart felt like it might beat out of my chest. I wanted to *fix* it. My hurt rapidly turned to anger when I realized I couldn't, and the only person who *could* fix it, wasn't. I knew it was a mistake when I took out my phone, I just didn't care. *You did say you'd text her.*

T: You're seriously letting him move?

T: Do you have any idea what it will do to his basketball prospects if he changes schools and isn't a starter?

T: Do you even fucking care?

T: Unbelievable. Your nose is so far in the air you can't even see that he's drowning.

I could have kept going. Somewhere, I knew none of it was her fault, but I couldn't stop.

. . .

V: I'd rather my nose be in the air than turning brown. Yours is so far up Luke's ass it's kind of embarrassing. I swear to you that if you do not lose my number, yours will be on every cougar-friendly dating site in existence. You'll have no time to hate-text me because your phone will be blowing up with offers from Lindas and Cheryls and other names of women who sound like they wear fringe and animal print together.

V: Fuck off.

I actually laughed out loud. And then I couldn't stop laughing. *You are so incredibly stupid*. Tears started to roll down my cheeks, and I realized I probably looked a little unstable, sitting in my parked car, somewhere between laughing and sobbing. Luke was going to kill me for being an ass to Vanessa *again*, and I didn't even know if I'd see him at school anymore. The whole wall of my precariously built façade was crumbling to the ground.

––––––

That night stretched on forever. I tried to imagine any possible excuse I could give that would let this entire thing blow over, and I came up short. I also didn't know how much longer I could go on hiding who I was from my best friend, even if that meant losing him. I had to pull over twice on the seven-minute drive to his house the next morning to think about throwing up. My stomach was not on board with the honesty plan.

When I got there, Luke's uncle answered and let me in. I supposed that was lucky, since Luke might have slammed the door in my face. I came to his door as he was packing, and I hated that he was leaving, even if just a few towns over.

"Hey," I said pathetically.

"Dude, you do not wanna have this conversation with me right now."

"I do, though. I know I was in the wrong. I thought—"

"I don't wanna hear about what you thought, Troy. I don't wanna hear about how you hate Vanessa or that you think I shouldn't be moving in with my uncle." Luke continued to shove things into a bag from wherever his eyes landed in his room.

"I know I screwed up with Vanessa *again*. I'll beg her for forgiveness, I don't care, but I can't stand you being this pissed at me. I just don't think you should have to leave when it's not something you did. It's not fair." *And I am so afraid you'll leave for good*, I wanted to add on. I knew he wasn't changing schools, at least not yet, but it felt like a big deal.

"Good luck with V. She's not the forgiving type. And huge shocker, I know, but life's not fair. Oh, well. Here's where I am, and this is what I'm doing."

"Okay. Yeah. Okay, I get what you're saying... I just..." Luke finally stopped moving and really *looked* at me. I felt the color drain from my face.

"Dude, are you okay? You kind of look like you're going to puke, and I gotta be honest that I can't deal with that right now."

I let out a laugh. "I don't know. I might."

"Damn it, Troy. Do you need a ride to the doctor or something?"

"No. I'm fine. Well, I'm terrified, but I'm fine."

"Is this like a riddle? I have shit to do, so could you get on with it? I'm not trying to be a dick, seriously, I just need to get out—"

"I'm gay." Once the words left my mouth, I didn't know if they were real. The whole thing felt like a scenario I'd gone over in my head too many times, and the air seemed to freeze while I waited for a reaction.

"You're gay."

"Yeah."

"Okay... I might be suffering from some sort of stress-induced stroke here, but what does your being gay have to do with anything we were just talking about?"

"It's just... it's not that I don't *get* your life when I say I don't want you to move. I just don't want you to." My feet wouldn't stay still in that moment. There was too much truth hanging in the atmosphere around my head, and none of it would land until Luke said *something*. He was quiet, but I saw reality light up in his green eyes.

"T... man, you know I love you like a brother. Even if you drive me completely insane."

"Yeah. Like a brother." Even though it was the answer I knew I'd get, it cut me somewhere deep. Before he'd said it, the possibility still existed in some alternate reality. But now...

"I'm sorry I don't... I mean, I'm in love with Vanessa, but it's not just because of her. I don't feel that way." My best friend looked incredibly uncomfortable, which was my cue to leave. At least he wasn't kicking me out.

"It's cool. I assumed you didn't, I just... I don't know. I needed to explain what my insanity has been about, I guess. If you could not, like, tell everybody about this—" It was worth a shot to at least try to keep my private life private until graduation.

"Troy, come on, man. I wouldn't. I don't care that you're gay, either. Not that I have some sort of right to have an opinion, either way... it just doesn't have to change anything, like us being friends."

Yeah. Right. I didn't know that anything could ever be normal between us, or that it had been *normal* ever. Not when Luke had no idea how I felt about him since we met. *Maybe all of it was fake.* I knew that was a lie, but it seemed like it might be easier to say goodbye to him if I believed we were never really friends to begin with.

"Thanks. For saying that. Good luck moving." I nodded and headed out of the room. I'd spent so much time planning and thinking about that conversation, but I didn't really have any type of plan for what to do now.

———

I drove home in a fog. I felt like something was missing, but I wasn't sure if it felt *bad* or not. It took some convincing from my brain that I had actually just come out to Luke, and everything was more or less okay. Not in the sense that I got anything I wanted, but that he didn't freak out. There was a weird cocktail of hurt and pride going on in my chest. Hearing him say he didn't want me was painful. Not that I hadn't anticipated it, but the words were different in reality than in my head.

I pulled into my driveway and sat in my car, waiting for my hands to stop shaking all the way. Besides the hollow feeling in my chest about not knowing if Luke and I could ever be friends again like before, there was also a lightness that came with letting go of the *fear* of telling him. *It's over. You actually did it.* Things still sucked, but the whole situation made me think about what else I could do, if I really wanted it. It was a kind of fear that left me feeling exhilarated rather than defeated.

It was a start.

Continued in Me, Myself? and Manaia

Read more about Luke and Vanessa in Nicole Campbell's Gem City Series

In your opinion, what mistakes were made in this story?

_____

_____

_____

_____

_____

Which character(s) could have done something differently in the process of figuring out these intense feelings?

_____

_____

_____

_____

_____

What advice would you give Troy about how to move forward? Luke?

_____

_____

_____

_____

_____

Is there anything Troy could say to Vanessa to make things right? What would it take?

_____

_____

_____

_____

_____

Do you think things will really stay the same between Troy and Luke?

_____

_____

_____

_____

_____

Do you think Luke will tell Vanessa about Troy? How would Luke and Troy's friendship be affected?

_____

_____

_____

_____

_____

What can you take away from this story?

_____

Thoughts:

ABUSE AND OTHER A WORDS: A STORY IN THREE VIGNETTES

ONE

"Hey, baby," a light-haired boy called across the gas station parking lot to me. *Shit*. I said nothing and willed the tank to be full already. It was late, and I'd almost attempted to coast home on fumes rather than stopping to fill up, but now I was here.

Said guy started sauntering over toward my car, and I couldn't quite make the decision quickly enough about whether or not I should get back into the car and wait him out, and he approached me before I moved.

"You can't talk?" He grinned again and leaned on the gas pump casually.

"'Can't' and 'don't want to' aren't the same things," I replied, finally making eye contact. I stopped the pump manually and hoped he didn't see my hands shake.

"Well, I was going to tell you that you were looking good, but now I know you're a bitch, so thanks for saving me the trouble."

I just looked at him again, afraid to open my car door while he was still so close to me.

"Thanks for the apology, have a great fucking night." He pushed off the pump and walked back to his truck, leaving me to shove the nozzle back in, fall into my seat, and lock the doors. Shaking out my hands, I made myself wait until his car was gone before I rolled out onto the road.

Did this guy do anything wrong? If so, what? If not, why was the girl fearful?

_____

_____

_____

_____

_____

How (if at all) does the impression of this story change depending on whether the reader is male or female?

_____

_____

_____

_____

_____

Thoughts:

_____

_____

_____

_____

_____

TWO

The skin below my fingernail, or what used to be my fingernail, was starting to bleed. I sat in the most public table possible at the coffee shop, hoping Tara would keep her shit together in order to avoid a scene. It wasn't going to work, but it was at least an attempt. I continued to chew on my finger anyway, knowing she was on her way there and already suspicious that I said I couldn't pick her up. *This is going to be so incredibly bad.*

I tried re-arranging sugar packets in the container on the table to keep my brown eyes focused somewhere other than the parking lot. I hadn't slept well since I'd decided I had to break up with my girlfriend five days ago. Really, five months ago, but five days ago was when I decided I didn't care anymore what the consequences were. I had to be done. *Just get out the words and leave. Do not get sucked in.* She had a way of twisting a situation. I'd decided that five days ago was the last time I'd let her do it.

I moved from the sugar packets to the salt and pepper shakers. I knew she was late on purpose. Everything was calculated. I didn't know how she did it, but I did know that somehow I ended up apologizing to her and promising to do better after I found out she was hooking up with a guy in her drama class. *Like she needs a freaking class.*

The door chimed and Tara floated in, her red hair trailing behind her. "Hey, babe. Sorry I'm late. I guess I'm just not used to doing things so last-minute." She smiled and sat down across from me.

Jab number one, and I haven't even said anything yet. "No problem. Did you want something to drink?"

"Well, it is a coffee shop." She smiled again, but a beat too late for it to feel natural.

"Right. Be right back." I stood in line wish I'd just blurted it out when she walked in. At least I had the forethought to order iced coffee in case it ended up being thrown in my face.

I set the coffee down in front of her and debated whether or not to sit or keep standing.

"Why are you being weird? Sit down." So I did, and I even hated that.

"Listen, Tara. I've been thinking a lot—"

"Wow, this should be good then."

"Yeah, okay. I'm done going out with you. I'll see you around." I scooted the chair back, relief having not yet arrived. Not until I was out of there.

"*Sit your ass down*," Tara hissed. I didn't. So that was a start, but I did stall and look down at her.

"If this is about Bryan, I can't even believe you would bring that back up after we already discussed what I need from you to keep that from happening again."

"No. *You* discussed. What *I* need for that not to happen again is for us to not be together anymore." *You're getting sucked in. Just walk away.*

"That's awesome, Josh. I've given you *everything* and you're just going to break up with me in the middle of a Starbucks? I don't even know what to say to that." The tears she was so adept at producing came right on cue, and I resumed my path towards the door. "Maybe you'll realize what you had once I'm dead. Or maybe you won't care at all." She mumbled it just perfectly so that she knew I heard it, but not so loud that everyone would stare.

There was a part of me who needed to stop and turn and make her explain the comment. But the part of me that was just so sick of all the mind games and the threats and the pit in my stomach knew I had to keep walking. *It's not your job to save her.* That was something my mom had said maybe three thousand times since I started dating Tara, and I was glad it stuck. I put one foot in front of the other, took my phone out of my pocket to block her number, and hoped to God I was free.

Do you consider Josh and Tara's relationship to be abusive? In what way?

_____

_____

_____

_____

_____

Did Josh handle Tara's allusion to committing suicide in the right way? What would you have done in his place? What are some possible motivations for Tara to say that?

_____

_____

_____

_____

_____

Thoughts:

_____

_____

_____

_____

_____

———

THREE

I clutched the piece of paper in my hand as I walked into

school, afraid if I let it go it might disappear. It felt like my own personal Hogwarts letter— the letter that held the key to me getting out of my foster mom's house and away from *Tom*. I made a face just thinking about Deidre's boyfriend while I opened my locker. I put the letter between my teeth for safekeeping and grabbed my books for my first two periods.

"Mari!" I heard my best friend call.

"Wshp," I tried to get out with the paper between my lips.

"Was that English?" Rebecca asked as she walked up. "A little morning snack?" She cocked her head to the side and let her long brown hair fall around her shoulder.

I swung my locker shut.

"I'm too excited to even care how lame that was. Because *this* came this morning!" I waved the opened envelope in her face, and she grabbed it.

"You got in?!" She quickly pulled out the first page from the envelope and skimmed. "Oh my god. You got in! To UCSD!"

"I got in! And that's not even the best part!"

Her eyes looked up from the letter. "You got the grant?"

"Girl... I got the Hope Grant, the NFPA Scholarship, plus four others from some of the twenty-five thousand organizations where I applied for funding. It's happening." My eyes started swimming with tears, and Rebecca threw her arms around me.

"Whoa, who ordered girl-on-girl action?" Michael's voice interrupted behind us.

"So funny," I replied, wiping my eyes.

"No really, what's up?" He shot a look at Becca, and she started down the hallway with a wave.

"Babe. I got in to UCSD with almost complete tuition and housing assistance." My voice still almost broke when I said it out loud.

"Sweet."

"Sweet? Yeah, I'd say the chance to go to school and have someplace to live is pretty sweet. Jesus." I bit my lip, wishing he could be excited for once in his freaking life. I tucked my hair behind my ears and stuck the admissions envelope into my binder.

"Don't get so worked up, Mari. It's great. It's just a state school, that's all."

"A great state school, yeah."

"All I'm saying is that you could do better, honestly."

"I could do better than almost a full ride to UCSD?"

"Well, a full ride to Stanford would be better, yeah. And a full ride you actually earned. But I already said it was sweet. You don't need to fly off the handle—"

"A full ride I actually earned? What does that mean?"

"Like for grades, or sports or something, I don't know. You got yours because you're a foster kid and you're Mexican. It's cool, it's just not the same."

"I'm Guatemalan." I hated that my voice was smaller than my anger. We'd been dating for six months, and he knew full well my background.

"You know what I mean. Are you seriously going to be a bitch about me telling you it's sweet that you got into UCSD?" His dark eyes narrowed at me, a look I was accustomed to. Everything I found attractive about Michael— the dark eyes and the big smile, it all faded when he looked at me like that.

"You said I didn't earn it." The hallway was filling up quickly, and I assumed it was minutes to the first bell. "And you *know* how hard I worked—"

"You could have just said 'yes Michael, I'm going to over-react and be a bitch because you said *sweet* to me about UCSD,' and I would have walked away already. I'll see you when you've calmed down."

He shoved his hands in the pockets of his jeans and saun-tered towards his first class, having sucked all the joy out of my moment.

There is a form of common verbal abuse called "trivializ-ing," whereby one partner makes the other partner's accomplishments seem insignificant. Is this what Michael is doing here? If yes, why? If not, what is he doing?

_____

_____

_____

_____

_____

How could a relationship where trivializing occurs consistently affect the person on the receiving end of the abuse?

_____

_____

_____

_____

_____

Thoughts:

_____

_____

_____

_____

_____

YOUR TURN: PERSONAL JOURNAL
RELATIONSHIP IDEALS AND VALUES

Make a list of things you wish for in a relationship and/or what qualities you value in a significant other. Then, make a few bullet points as to why this is important to you. In the section on the next page, make note of any thoughts you have that you worry may be different than the thoughts of the important people in your life: parents, significant others, friends— anyone whose opinion might influence yours, and think about how you would handle that conversation. You don't have to have the answers right now. This exercise is about thinking ahead and understanding how you really feel.

Possible Conflicts & Thoughts:

_____

_____

_____

_____

_____

_____

_____

_____

_____

_____

_____

_____

_____

_____

_____

_____

Currently, how are you feeling in your decisions? Do you need more time to think? Do you need to consult someone you trust? Or are you feeling like you have a handle on what you want? A 1 would be not at all confident, and a 5 would be extremely confident.

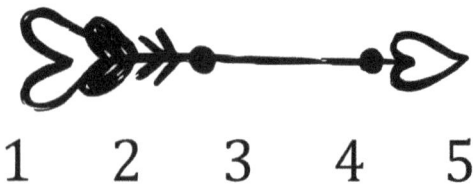

1   2   3   4   5

Important decisions take a lot of thought and consideration. This is why we're doing this! Most (not all) young adults have a working knowledge of the mechanics of sex and STDs from a high school Sex Education or Human Growth and Development course. Some states and counties do not even do this, however, and you can be left in the dark. Our focus here is the skill set to build a relationship beyond the basics, but if you have not had a comprehensive education in sex or human development, please check out: kidshealth.org or stayteen.org.

Right now, it's important that you honestly assess where you are in your comfort level regarding discussing big decisions in relationships. This could include your physical relationship, your expectations, your fears, and your goals. A lot of these topics seem like they would be awkward to discuss, but what is honestly more awkward is to have to make a decision for which you aren't adequately prepared.

On a scale of 1-10, rate below the level of comfort you have in your knowledge of these topics, as well as your comfort level in asking for more information about these topics, if needed. Make notes for yourself about any areas you find particularly awkward or uncomfortable, and try to come up with at least one trusted source you could discuss it with (doctor, parent, nurse, a credible health website like those listed above, etc).

Topic	Knowledge	Comfort
Basic Sex Talk		
Consent & Reciprocity (equal benefit for each partner)		
What Qualities You Find Attractive & Why		
How to Decide Upon and Discuss Boundaries		
Personal Insecurities		
Sexual Harassment & Assault		
Safe Sex/Contraception		

Notes:

_____

_____

It seems backward that we can all discuss meaningless small talk with anyone we come across, but we feel awkward or embarrassed discussing real issues that impact real lives with people who are close to us. This first challenge is a big one, but I'd like you to look at your table from the previous page, and pick a topic you'd like to start with, and a person you'd like to talk to. Ideally, this person would have more life experience than you and is someone whom you know cares about your well-being. If you feel that you're in that place with your significant other, and you're ready to have a big conversation, this same planning piece could be used for that as well. Be open that you'd like to have a conversation, and let this person know how you're most comfortable communicating. There are some options listed below, but you could also come up with your own.

Coffee or Meal
Sometimes, it's helpful to get out of the house and be in a public place. You can choose somewhere that has somewhat private tables or areas, or even go on a picnic. This provides a neutral space for discussion.

Personal Space

Depending on your relationship with this person, being in your room or somewhere in your home may be more comfortable. For some, however, this may feel like an intrusion - you know yourself and you should trust your gut.

Written Conversation

In some cases, it may be necessary to work up to a face-to-face conversation. If you can't imagine talking about these things with anyone in your life, it may help to start a written conversation. This could be in the form of a journal or even via email. Just something where each of you can think about what you want to say and also have time to control your reactions to the other's comments. Make sure that you trust this person implicitly if you're putting things in writing.

Before any important conversation, whether with a parent, boyfriend, girlfriend, partner, whomever— it is good practice to have an idea of what you want to discuss first and the points you want to get across. This helps you stay on track and avoid becoming flustered or conceding to something when you don't want to. If you've decided to move forward in having one of these conversations, take this space to plan out your goals and feelings, and then take this list with you when the conversation occurs.

. . .

It may seem unnecessary to do this much work to have a conversation, but the issue becomes when one or both people involved are uncomfortable, and they tend to rush through things so it can be "over." And these are not the types of discussions to rush through— they're too important. At the same time, if a conversation becomes too much, don't be afraid to take a break and revisit soon. Make a plan for when that will happen.

Ideas & Notes:

Example: Sexual Assault – What does it really mean, is it different than rape? How could I handle unwanted attention? Or you could also discuss the stories you've read so far, etc.

Reflect on the success of your first structured conversation. Were there things that surprised you? Things you need to think about before your next conversation? Maybe you want to change up the setting of your meeting or you want to prepare differently. It can be helpful to share these ideas with whoever your chosen person is. If it was a difficult discussion, you might wait a few days and write down your ideas to share. The most important thing is that you are building new bridges with someone you trust and who cares about your well-being. This isn't about being told what to do — it's about really hearing what others, whom you believe have your best interests at heart, have to say, and considering those voices along with your own. *This* is what adulting is: making tough decisions, asking the right people for advice, and knowing yourself well enough to determine when it's right for you.

On a scale of 1-5, how successful was this conversation and why?

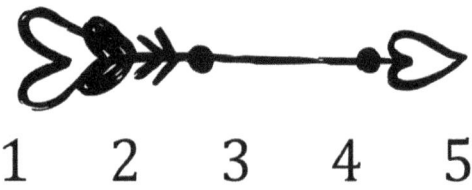

1 2 3 4 5

Notes:

_____

_____

_____

_____

_____

_____

_____

_____

_____

_____

_____

_____

_____

_____

_____

_____

_____

_____

_____

_____

_____

_____

_____

WHAT ARE YOU REALLY THINKING?

The more you act like a lady, the more he'll act like a gentleman

— Sydney Biddle Barrows

This is such a ridiculous thought. It's equally offensive to both genders. The way a female acts should not determine the way a male acts because we are all sentient beings with our own thoughts and values and rationale and.... well, you get the point.

———

There are so many ways that we avoid the "what are you really thinking" conversation. Maybe because we don't want to know what someone is really thinking. In our heads, their thoughts define us, and maybe not in a way we like. Or maybe, we have an idea of what they're thinking and if they say it out loud, it might "kill the mood." Maybe we're so blindsided we don't even know what *we're* thinking.

It is absolutely not your job to magically know what someone else is thinking, but if you're considering having any kind of relationship with that person (physical, emotional, both, casual, serious, somewhere in between), it is *absolutely* your job to ask. In the next section, we'll focus on the importance of knowing your own boundaries, but this section is really about how to determine someone else's boundaries and what consent looks like.

It is 100% your job to ask and then to accept the answer. And no, whether or not the other person is acting like a gentleman or a lady or *not* doesn't actually have to affect your behavior at all.

At the same time— if someone asks you if you're sure, if you're okay, if what is going on is all right— assume they're asking for the truth. If they're asking, they want to know your answer, not the answer you think you "should" give. Respect that person's right to have a mutually enjoyable experience (reciprocity).

<3 Nicole

CHEATER, CHEATER, PUMPKIN PIE EATER

I was one of those weird kids who actually got along with her sibling. Like, my brother was my best friend, and the house was really freaking depressing since he went away to school.

This was why I found myself sitting in my Jeep at the airport cell phone lot an hour and a half early. I couldn't sit still any longer, and waiting in my car was just as easy as waiting at home.

It was the week of Thanksgiving, and Wes would be landing within the hour. I just felt like things would be normal for the first time since August. I might have also been a little bit stoked for Carter to be home too, but as it was part of our unspoken agreement, I couldn't act like it was a big deal.

Carter was Wes's friend first, but the three of us got along so well as kids that I didn't even remember when it went from Wes and Carter to Wes, Carter, and me. I tapped my fingers on the steering wheel incessantly while pretending to listen to a podcast for AP Gov.

I jumped when my phone finally buzzed and practically tackled it.

Wes: We're here. I hope you brought snacks.

Cami: Of course I brought snacks. And we? Am I driving Carter too? I thought his mom was picking him up?

Wes: You're the best sister. He told his mom not to worry about it. Plus, she doesn't bring snacks. Now come get us.

I half-wished I'd bothered to put on makeup after my post-run shower that morning, but honestly, Carter had seen me in pretty much every stage of appearance possible. I just enjoyed the buzz across my skin as I put the Jeep in drive and headed toward the terminal.

———

The moment they'd jumped in the Jeep, it was like they'd never left. Other than the fact that Carter had a whole goatee thing going on that he hadn't before, everything felt the same. I hadn't realized I was nervous it would be different until that moment, like somehow, when they went to college they'd enter a different world. And yet, they were still arguing about who would play first on GTA.

"Are you really not going to go home first?" I asked.

"Are you *really* going to pretend you don't want me in your house as soon as possible so that you can soak in my awesomeness while you have the chance?" Carter reached up and pulled playfully on my ponytail. My brother gave him a look I couldn't quite decipher while I was driving, but I ignored it. I kind of did want to soak up Carter's awesomeness while I had the chance.

I pulled into our driveway after an epic Beastie Boys singalong, and it actually felt like home. I put the Jeep into park, but Carter touched my arm before I could shut it off. "Hey, I'm feeling kind of bad now about not stopping by my house. Do you think you could drop me at home?" His blue eyes actually did look a little guilty, and even though it was out of character, I figured he had been away from home for a while. I tried not to let the disappointment show on my face that we weren't going to get to hang out.

"Lame," Wes said, grabbing his bag. "Come by later. And I'm taking the rest of the snacks." He looked at us both seriously and did, in fact, grab the rest of the corn nuts and Hostess cupcakes from the console.

Carter hopped into the front seat as my brother disappeared into the house. I put the car into reverse. "Thank god *he's* gone," Carter joked. He leaned over and pressed his lips below my ear, sending a delicious shiver up my spine.

"Yes, always in the way, that brother of mine." I turned my head and let him kiss me for the first time since he got on a plane that August. His goatee felt different, but the kiss was familiar.

"I missed you, Cami."

"I missed you, too," I whispered, not wanting the tightness in my voice to show.

"Let's go to the beach before you take me home, yeah?"

"Because you want to listen to the waves?"

"Because I want to listen to the sounds you make when I touch you." I expected him to laugh after that, but he didn't. My cheeks warmed, and I drove in the direction of our favorite spot.

We didn't talk much on the drive. I tried to enjoy the moment of him tickling the palm of my hand as I drove, knowing he'd be gone in a matter of days. The beach was mostly empty as I pulled up— it was November and freaking cold, but we didn't really come for the weather anyway. "Come here," he requested quietly. I killed the engine and climbed over to his lap.

"Here I am."

"Closer."

I pressed my body as close to him as I could, relishing the warmth of his arms around me. "Better?"

"Slightly." He grinned and kissed me again, deeper this time, and I wondered if I wasn't alone in how much I'd missed him. "Is this okay? I didn't really ask, I just missed you..."

"Definitely okay," I said, proving it by kissing him again. We'd texted, but never anything serious. It was part of the agreement. We both knew we couldn't handle long-distance, so it was easier not to go there. Plus, we hadn't even been technically *together* before he left. But in this moment, when Carter's hands were tracing lines around my hips, I didn't want him to leave again.

The sun was on its last glimmer of light when Carter pulled back. "I probably should go home. Just for a bit."

"Yeah, probably. And my mother is probably having a stroke about the fact that I'm not helping make pies or something."

"Mmmm. Pie sounds good."

"Are you always hungry?"

"For pie? Yes. For you? Also yes." He smiled at me again, and I melted a little bit at his corniness. I pressed my lips to his cheek and reluctantly left his warmth, and drove him home.

———

I walked inside my house to find my brother and father on the couch watching ESPN and my mother in the kitchen.

"Oh, good, you're home. Roll out that pie crust, will you?" my mother asked immediately upon my arrival.

"What kind of anti-feminist agenda are you trying to promote here? I see two able-bodied humans sitting right there on the couch."

My mom rolled her eyes. "You can wear your pussy-hat while you roll the crust, if it makes you feel better. Your brother just got home, and your father hurts more than he helps in the kitchen, and you know it."

"I heard that!" my dad called from the couch.

"I meant you to!" my mom called right back.

"Fine, fine. I *am* going to wear the hat though."

———

Carter made good on his promise to come over that night, but it was mostly video games and Chinese take-out— Mom didn't cook for us the night before Thanksgiving. It was not exactly a romantic affair, but I appreciated that his hand found its way to mine often.

Wes knew about Carter and me, he just didn't want to *see* it. I got it. His PDAs with his ex made me want to vomit. So we kept it low-key. When Wes left to replenish our drinks, Carter folded his fingers with mine and leaned in. I tugged the sides of his shirt to bring him closer and leaned on the arm of the couch behind me. His hands were warm against my skin, and I just wanted more time. I didn't hear Wes walk in, but I did hear him clear his throat.

"Really? You couldn't walk slower?" Carter joked, taking a Dr. Pepper from my brother.

"No, I couldn't. And by the way, Raychel has texted me at least seven times because you haven't been responding. So maybe you take care of that."

"Seriously, bro?" Carter pulled back from me and glared at my brother.

"Seriously. Yeah." Wes sounded calm, but the look in his eyes was not. My gut twisted.

"I'll be right back, Cami."

"Uh, sure."

Carter grabbed his phone off the side table and shuffled out of the family room.

"What the hell, Wes?" I threw a pillow forcefully at my brother's head. Carter and I had discussed a sort of "don't ask" policy when it came to us dating other people. Unless it was serious, and then we'd tell the other. And Wes had just come and flash-flooded my parade.

"This is my fault?"

"Yes! Things were fine." I felt the tears spring up behind my eyes, and I was determined to keep them there.

"So you're cool with him sleeping with Raychel and making plans to *bring her home* over Christmas. You didn't want to know about that?"

"Stop it, Wes! Jesus! I don't want to hear this! Why are you trying to ruin this weekend?"

"Because he can't treat you like you don't matter, that's why. You might be fine with it, but I'm not. And I told him he had to tell you, or I would, so now I guess that makes me the asshole. Sorry." Wes chucked the remote to the TV across the couch and stormed out. As much as I tried to keep them in, the tears found their way down my cheeks. I got up to shut off the PlayStation; I just wanted to go to my room.

Carter came back as I was walking out. "Cami, wait. Please? Let me explain."

"Explain that you went back on our agreement? Explain that I'm going to have to sit across the table from *Raychel* when our families do Christmas Eve dinner? Explain when you were planning on mentioning it?"

"Fucking Wes."

"This isn't on him. This is on you." I swallowed back a sob and leaned against the wall.

"Cami... it's just... we talked about this, though, right? You and I... we aren't people who stay single. I miss you, and I won't bring Raychel home. It wasn't even a plan, she just mentioned it, and Wes happened to be there. I'm not, like, in love with her. It's just a casual... thing."

"It feels different when the casual thing has a name and is making plans to come home with you and meet your family. That doesn't feel casual." My voice was calmer, but the tears still made themselves known.

"Cami," he said, stepping into my space and rubbing my arms. "I swear to you, I didn't go back on our agreement. This isn't anything serious. If it was, I would have told you, and I told Wes the same damn thing." It was harder to be mad when he was touching me.

"I don't know that I can talk about this anymore tonight. I want to un-know it."

"Then can't we just do that? Nothing has changed. I'm sorry."

"What did you say to her on the phone?" The words felt wrong coming out of my mouth. Up until that point, she was the *other* girl, but that made it sound like *I* was.

"That I was here with my family and friends, and I'd see her at school. That's it. Because it's *nothing*."

"But you're sleeping with her?"

Carter's eyes didn't leave mine, but he didn't say anything. "Is that a deal breaker? We can't do this thing with us if I'm hooking up with someone else at school?"

"I honestly don't know. I hadn't gone there in my head." I *knew* he would date, I knew he'd hook up. He was one of the flirtiest guys I knew. I always just thought maybe I'd be the exception, and that was a dangerous thing to think.

"I'm just going to go to bed."

"Let me come and lie with you. We don't have to talk about it, and we don't have to do anything. Just don't make me walk away. Please. Damn it, I mean, I will if you want me to, I just want you to know I don't want to." His hands were still on my arms, though they'd stopped moving. He was looking at me with a question in his eyes. The image of him getting on a plane in three days and the image of him being with some other girl were competing in my mind. I nodded and said nothing, hoping that he'd follow but not wanting to say that out loud. He did.

———

I'd tried to close my eyes and fall asleep, but it was difficult with him lying beside me. Tears kept welling up and then subsiding, and Carter would rub my back when I couldn't hold them in.

"Cami?"

"You said we didn't have to talk."

"I did. I just... I need to know what you're thinking. I'm dying over here."

"What I'm thinking... is that this is so fucking unfair. It sounds so stupid, but I was here first, and now I have to feel.... like *this*, when.... I don't know. It's not fair." I flipped over to face him, and that was a bad idea. His eyes were red too, and I hadn't realized that he'd been crying.

"I'm sorry."

"Ugh, but why should you be? You didn't make me any promises. Just... did you make her any?"

"No. I know that I'm not big on commitment, but I'm not *that* guy either. You know that."

"We're really killing it with this friends with benefits things, you know?" I managed a smile at that.

"Oh, absolutely. Smooth sailing."

"If things change... if you start making promises..."

"I will tell you. Even if it kills me, I'll tell you."

"Then I'll believe you tonight. Even if it kills me, I'll believe you. Please don't make me regret it."

"I won't. I swear."

"And Wes?"

"I'll talk to him."

"Maybe I'll talk to him first. But that's for tomorrow."

"And tonight?" he asked.

I let my fingers travel up his chest and around the back of his neck, I let the familiarity of him and me take hold of my heart, and I let myself hope I wouldn't be hating myself over pumpkin pie the next day.

How do you feel about this overall situation? Who do you find yourself identifying with or agreeing with?

_____

_____

_____

_____

_____

In getting to know Cami, do you think she will have regrets about continuing to have this non-relationship with Carter?

_____

_____

_____

_____

_____

Is Wes right to interfere and tell his sister about Raychel?

_____

_____

_____

_____

_____

We don't know much about Raychel, and we have two accounts of her relationship with Carter. How do you think this would affect her?

_____

_____

_____

_____

_____

If Raychel and Cami don't have all of the truth, can there really be consent between either of them and Carter?

_____

_____

_____

_____

_____

What can you take away from this story?

_____

_____

_____

_____

_____

. . .

Thoughts:

_____

_____

_____

_____

_____

_____

_____

_____

_____

FRIENDS OR FOES?

** Trigger Warning: Sexual Assault/Rape **

I felt like I owned this town. Okay, that might have been a slight exaggeration, but it was my first trip back since I'd left for college. It had only been six weeks, but I felt different. I let the warm air slide under my fingers as I rode shotgun in my best friend Shea's Civic.

"Ohhhhh, let's get a Slurpee!" she yelled as she grabbed my wrist.

"I thought Slurpees were for bad days. And *this* is not a bad day. This is a great day." We'd been driving without a purpose for the last twenty minutes since she picked me up at my parents'. *See? It's not even 'my house' anymore... completely weird.*

"Slurpees can be for any reason, Em. Don't act like you don't know that."

"Fine, fine. Then what?"

"There's a party-ish at Seth's tonight."

"A party-ish?"

"Like ten, twelve people. Nothing crazy. I think his brother and some of his friends are in town too, but Brian will be there, and that's a good enough reason for me."

"You're still on that? Aren't you dating—"

"Shhhhh, lalalalalalala I can't hear you." Shea stuck her fingers in her ears as we sat at the light before 7-Eleven. I let out a laugh. Some things didn't change.

"Okay. Brian. Got it. Maybe the four years of flirting will become something magical." She side-eyed me without hesitation and pulled into the parking lot. She was out of the car and in the store within seconds, her long mocha colored hair swinging behind her. I used to do whatever I could to get my hair to lay like that – chemical straighteners, every product on the planet. Now that my hair was natural, I loved it. I also wasn't the only black girl at my college like I was here, so that might have helped, too. I made my way into the store and filled a cup with kiwi-strawberry icy deliciousness. Shea was already halfway done with her blue raspberry drink and holding the bridge of her nose in pain.

"So cold. So so so cold." Her petite face was scrunched up, and I sighed.

"You are acting like a Slurpee newbie. Get it together," I said sternly.

"You're right." Shea blinked and took a deep breath before resuming her naturally occurring fierce-face.

"To Seth's, then?" I asked while we paid.

"Changing clothes… then Seth's."

I groaned. That added at least forty minutes, plus more, if she tried to make me wear something of hers. "You look great. No changing clothes," I pleaded.

"Yes. For both of us. You can't be walking in looking all high school."

"I'm okay with a T-shirt and jeans. You can change if you really want to, but I'm not—" I was interrupted by blue-raspberry Slurpee flying from Shea's straw to the middle of my white T-shirt.

"Oops."

"You… are a bitch."

She only smiled bigger at that as I dabbed fruitlessly at the bright blue stain. "I'll throw it in the wash at my house and you can borrow something."

I glared at her victorious face and resigned myself to my fate.

———

I was feeling a little smug when we walked into Seth's house. I'd found almost an identical t-shirt in a turquoise color in Shea's closet. *Ha.*

I'd always liked Seth's house- it was open, airy, and it smelled like laundry detergent. Everyone was out back by the pool and maybe two beers ahead. I knew mostly everyone well, except for Seth's older brother Jake and a couple of his friends. I caught the name Matt, but I didn't imagine I'd need to remember it. I stopped a bit short when I saw Angel. As much shit as I gave Shea about her endless flirtation with Brian, I had sort of a similar situation with Angel in high school. Nothing ever happened, really. A school dance here or there with our friends, but he was always a *maybe someday* for me.

"I saved you a spot," he called to me once all of the *hey, how's school?* small talk died down.

"I don't see an extra chair. Unless you're planning on giving me yours?" I couldn't help smiling at him. His skin looked like caramel and there was always a grin on his face. He'd apparently gotten glasses, and this did nothing to dampen his cute factor.

"I didn't say *chair*, I said *spot*." He opened his arms and pointed to his lap.

"Presumptuous much?" I tried to look offended and put my hand on my hip, but I couldn't help laughing instead. He pulled me onto his lap and wrapped his arms around me from behind.

"Cariño, where you been?"

"Like you're not stalking my Instagram. You know exactly where I've been."

"It's possible." He smirked. "Let me get you a drink— you want a beer?"

"She'll have vodka," Shea interjected.

"I won't have vodka, thanks. A beer is fine." I started to get up since he said he was going to get it for me, but he only hugged me tighter and rested his chin on my shoulder.

"Seth! Bring *mi sirenita* a beer!"

"You've picked up new lines since I saw you last." I laughed.

"You know it."

"I like the glasses too, by the way. You look—"

"Like a really sexy Mexican Harry Potter? Yeah, I get that a lot."

"You took the words right out of my mouth." A beer appeared in my hand, and other than replenishing my food or drink, Angel stayed close all night. His hands felt good on my skin, and I started to regret the fact that we'd never tried to be more when we were in school together. Not that three hours was that far, but things weren't the same after high school.

"I missed you," I murmured into his ear after we finished the world's longest game of poker. I was buzzed enough that I said it without fear. *Maybe there is some benefit to being out of high school*. I wasn't worried that he'd act weird on Monday.

"I missed you too, Em." His lips brushed across my neck and made my arms break out in goose bumps.

"Are you gonna stay over?" *Not at all obvious*. I was just tired of waiting for the things I wanted instead of taking them. I could see Shea across the patio pulling Brian inside. *Like that*.

"Nah, not tonight, I can't. I have to help my dad at the restaurant at the ass-crack of dawn. I actually should have left already."

I knew my face must have fallen. I didn't have great control over my expressions, even when I wasn't tipsy. "Gotcha."

"Hey, not because I don't want to. How long are you here? You wanna go out tomorrow?"

"Out?"

"Yeah, *out*."

"Like, just you and me?"

He let out a laugh. "Yeah, just you and me. I feel like an ass that I never asked you before."

"You are a little bit of an ass." Angel laughed and pressed his lips against my jaw.

"I'll make it up to you." A delicious shiver went up my spine as he slid me off of his lap. "You need a ride? I've got an Uber coming."

"That's okay. I'll crash on the couch until Shea decides she's ready to go."

"All right. I'll text you tomorrow."

"Kay. It was good to see you."

I sighed involuntarily as he walked back in the house and disappeared. I could still feel his lips on my skin, and I hoped he meant it that he'd text. Downing the rest of my drink, a part of me was afraid he wasn't into me like that, but I tried to hold onto some optimism. Mostly everyone had gone home or disappeared into the house somewhere in the last hour. The clock read two a.m., and I decided the sofa in the front room was calling my name.

———

I wasn't sure what time it was when my eyes tried to open, but I felt like I couldn't breathe. I sucked in air and tried to get my bearings when I remembered where I was. The room was a little off its axis, and there was someone breathing loudly in my ear.

"What..." I croaked. *Angel?*

"Shhhh, it's fine. It's me." It was dark, and I wasn't totally sure who *me* was, but I was now certain that my jeans were pushed down around my knees.

"I don't-" I started as I turned to roll over and get a grip on the situation, but his mouth was on mine and his tongue down my throat before I could finish. *Jake?* I'd known Seth's brother as long as I'd known Seth, but we weren't friends, or... anything. He was heavy. *Did I flirt with him? What time is it? Did Shea leave me here?* He sat up for a moment and I sucked in a deep breath. "Jake? Jake—" my voice was so scratchy, and I didn't know what I was supposed to say. I just wanted to go home.

"It's okay, I've got protection. Just relax." He pushed my underwear aside and was back on top of me, inside of me. His breath in my ear made me want to throw up. I squeezed my eyes shut and dug my nails into my palms. *Just be over, just be over, just be over.*

And then it was. "That was great," he murmured. He kissed my cheek and my neck and in between my breasts before dressing himself and going to his room, I assumed. My hands were shaking, my legs were shaking, and I could still feel his weight on me, making it hard to breathe. *Why did I do that? Why didn't I say no? How did that even happen?* I wanted to crawl out of my skin, and I really really wanted to just fucking breathe. I knew Jake wasn't some sort of, like, assaulter, but I didn't understand how we had come to be in that position or what had even happened. I just wanted to go home and sleep in my own bed. I re-dressed myself and got an Uber. My legs still shook as I walked outside to wait on the curb. I didn't want to walk around the house to find Shea and run into Jake, or find myself in the wrong room. *You should have left when Angel did.* The thought of Angel made my stomach threaten to let everything go. *Will he know? Is he going to hate me?* I'd wanted to go out with him… and then… I didn't know.

———

I got in the Uber and put on my seatbelt. About two minutes into the drive, I got a text.

Shea: Hey slut, did you leave?! What happened with Angel?

The air got hard to suck in again, and a tear worked its way down my cheek. *Everything's fine. You drank too much and hooked up. It happens.*

Me: Yeah. I was tired and I didn't know if you were going to stay all night. Nothing happened.

Shea: Well call me tomorrow!

Me: I will.

I just needed to shower and sleep and this would all just be a party story one day. *Remember that time I slept with Seth's brother?* But that just forced more tears out. I didn't know what to do to make this feeling go away.

———

Waking up was not my friend. I'd let myself cry in the shower the night before, but managed to convince myself it'd seem better in the morning. I checked my phone before the events of the previous night set in.

Shea: Holy shit, did you sleep with Jake? How the hell did that happen?

Oh god, no, no, no. If Shea knew, then Brian knew, and then Angel would know. And the following text confirmed that nightmare.

Angel: Hey... did something happen after I left last night? I thought we had a thing going on. Were you just pissed that I had to go? Because that's sort of a shitty thing to do.

· · ·

I set my phone down and picked it back up at least six hundred times. I didn't know what to say, but my brain wouldn't let me ignore it.

Me: I don't know... I wasn't pissed that you left, we did have a thing. I didn't mean to do anything. I don't know.

The tears came freely now, and my stomach made good on the promise to expel its contents. I sat on my bathroom floor and waited for the reply.

Angel: You didn't mean to have sex with someone after you told me

you wanted to go out? That's an awesome excuse. I'll see you around.

Me: I'm so sorry...

I didn't know what else to say. I didn't want to make Jake sound like a creeper, and I knew I should have done something, said something, anything.

I closed my eyes and wished to go back in time as more tears found their way down my cheeks.

Continued in *Angel and My Demons*

Was there consent between Emma and Jake? What does consent sound like or look like in a healthy experience? In this situation?

_____

_____

_____

_____

_____

Why do you think Emma pushes back against the idea that Jake has done something wrong?

_____

_____

_____

_____

_____

If you were Emma's friend, what would you say to her if she told you the whole story? What do you think Shea would have said?

_____

_____

_____

_____

_____

Did Jake believe he had consent? Explain your thinking.

_____

_____

_____

_____

_____

Do you think women perceive this story differently than men, or not?

_____

_____

_____

_____

_____

What do you hope you would have done if in a similar situation?

_____

_____

_____

_____

_____

What role did alcohol play in this story? Or do you feel that it wouldn't have mattered one way or another?

_____

_____

_____

_____

_____

What can you take away from this story?

_____

_____

_____

_____

_____

Thoughts:

(This is a really heavy story. You might want to come back to it after you work through the journal section)

_____

_____

_____

_____

_____

_____

_____

_____

_____

_____

_____

_____

_____

_____

_____

_____

YOUR TURN: PERSONAL JOURNAL
DO ASK AND DO TELL

Think about a time when you would have given anything to know what someone else was thinking. Reflect on why you needed to know, what was so important about it? Did you ask them? If not, what were you afraid of?

Situation:

_____

_____

_____

_____

_____

Why did you need to know?

_____

_____

_____

_____

_____

Did you ask the person? If yes, what happened? If no, why not?

_____

_____

_____

_____

_____

If you did eventually find out that person's thoughts on the situation, were they what you imagined?

_____

_____

_____

_____

_____

Which is worse: obsessing over what someone else is thinking, or biting the bullet and asking? Why?

_____

_____

_____

_____

_____

Take a minute here to brainstorm what you know about consent, any questions you have, and anything you think would be "weird" or "awkward" about having that conversation with someone.

_____

_____

_____

_____

_____

_____

_____

_____

_____

_____

_____

Consent:
Get it, Give It, Maintain It

Consent is in the media a lot, and for a good reason. The dictionary defines consent as: permission for something to happen or agreement to do something. It's a very simple concept, but these are things we hear:

- *I thought she wanted it.*
- *I didn't want her to think I was a pussy.*
- *All guys want sex.*
- *Well, what was she wearing?*

The list could go on, but you've heard it all before. The thing that doesn't get talked about as much is that consent isn't just about random hookups or casual relationships. Even if you've been in a relationship for years— you need to know that the other person is into what's going on. Every. Single. Time.

The five Ws on this one are easy:

Who

You. And every person you may ever be involved with.

What

Consent. Permission. See above for full definition.

. . .

Where

Anywhere and Everywhere.

When

Anytime you are thinking of being physical with another person.

Why

So many reasons, but because one human does not have the right to take away another human's choice about when/how/where to be touched.

Special Note: Someone who is under the influence of a mind-altering substance or is not conscious is not able to give consent. Period.

All of this information needs to be embedded into human DNA or something, but the last one is where our focus lies: *How?*

How is another question all together. And happily, this one doesn't have to be awkward. Asking for and giving consent can be romantic, it can be hot. But what it *can't* be is non-existent, coerced, or assumed.

Before

Ask for it verbally and **make sure the other person is comfortable saying "no."**

"Hey, are you okay with this? Do you want to keep going?"

"I don't want to do anything you're not good with, so if you want to slow down, it's okay. What would you like to do instead?"

Be ready to accept the answer. If it's "no," it's not a personal attack against you. It's a decision that is personal to them, and you need to be ready to try to understand from his or her point of view. Let them know it's okay, and you want them to be open with you.

If the answer is yes...

During

Communicate while things are happening between the two of you. Read body language and don't be afraid to speak up. It's important for both people to enjoy themselves (reciprocity).

- "Does that feel good? Can you tell me/show me what feels good?"
- "I like _____. Could we try _____?"
- Be aware if the other person looks uncomfortable

or is tense. You can ask if he or she wants to take a break or stop, and respect that answer. Being physical with someone should be pleasurable, not scary. If it's scary, something isn't right.

After

This piece is so important, and it doesn't just refer to immediately after. One or both people might have experienced something new. They may need to process how they're feeling, so do ask again later.

- "Was that okay? Is there anything you would want to do differently?"
- Could I do anything differently?
- Consent once is not consent always. You need to repeat these steps. People can change their minds, or you can change your mind. You don't owe anyone anything, and no one owes you anything. Period.

Remember

Silence is not consent. If you had to talk someone into something, it's not consent. If you do not have consent, it is sexual assault or rape. It's not "no big deal." It's a very, very big deal. More info at teachconsent.org

. . .

Rate your comfort level on a scale of 1-5 regarding asking for and/or giving consent:

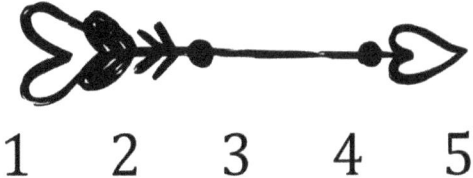

1   2   3   4   5

IS THIS EVEN HEALTHY?

While it's absolutely true that experience is the best teacher, it can often be the cruelest teacher as well. There is something to be said for figuring out what "normal" or "healthy" looks like *for you* before you are in a position where you're making that decision on the fly. There are a lot of situations that are looked at as "no big deal" or "normal" by what seems like everyone. That does not mean that standard has to apply to you. This book is not a cautionary tale about being a lady or a gentleman or what is "appropriate," because *only you* can decide that for yourself. Some people are very comfortable with casual situations, and others are not. The problem becomes when you try to make yourself do something that is not right for you, or accept something as normal that you know in your gut is *not* normal for you, and that's what is important to determine ahead of time.

Please, please, *please* know that if something has or ever does happen, it was and is not your fault. My hope is that knowing yourself and what you're okay with will allow you to understand that it is your right to demand that those boundaries be respected, and, if they're not, that it is your right to report it without an ounce of shame. It is also your right to learn from your own experiences and decide if you want to change your mind about what you're comfortable with.

The purpose of the following stories is to help you think about some of these things before you're faced with them or faced with them again. There are no right answers and there is no way to *know* exactly how you would react in a similar situation, but making sure you have a support system (someone to call or talk to) when you're feeling unsure or if you know something just isn't right is a really great tool to have in place.

I want to warn you that the story *Friends or Foes* can be triggering for anyone who has experience a sexual assault, so please proceed in whatever way is best for you, and please see the resources at the end of this book for where to get help dealing with that experience.

<3 Nicole

BIG FISH, SMALL POND

I'd had a two-hour layover in St. Louis before I made it to my destination. Thirteen 7-Ups, two failed attempts to start a new book, and one trashy magazine allowed me to make it through the first leg of my flight without crying next to a random stranger with a T-shirt that smelled like a moldy washing machine. The constant getting up to pee helped keep my mind off of the fact that my boyfrie... ex-boyfriend hadn't even seemed the slightest bit put off that I was leaving for the summer. *He sucks. He's a cheater. He's not even good at* anything *related to relationships.*

That was one of the new mantras I was trying. I didn't think it was working. It wasn't really that I was sad about *him*. I mean, I was. There were a lot of firsts and a lot of really good memories wrapped up in Chris. The footage posted all over Instagram with his tongue down some random girl's throat at a party he said he wasn't going to? That wasn't one of those memories. That made my insides feel like they were leading a rebellion.

I didn't feel much better about that fact that I'd still really expected him to get down on his knees and beg for forgiveness when I told him it was over. Or to ask me to stay when I told him (via my best friend Claire) that I was leaving for the summer to work for my uncle in This-Is-The-Smallest-Town-In-America. Though Claire tried to make it sound like there was regret swimming in his eyes... there wasn't. He didn't give a shit, and I was trying so hard not to.

As I sat in the luxurious vinyl chair waiting for my second flight, the tears came. No amount of gum or cheap airport cookies or angry playlists in my ears made them stop. *Fuck him. Fuck him. Fuck him.* God I wanted to hate him, and his stupid hair that was always an inch too long, and the way he never chewed pizza with his mouth all the way closed. But as I said... it wasn't that I missed *him*— I missed everything I'd put into him— our relationship. It was all gone, and I didn't know how to get it back.

"I'm ninety-seven percent sure it'll be fine," Claire had said before I left. "You'll probably meet a guy who bales hay or something and has a six pack and you'll be the 'big city' girl, and he'll fall in love with you." She had a way of saying ridiculous things with a completely matter-of-fact tone. That three percent of uncertainty was weighing on me now, but it was too late to go home.

———

It was humid. I'd known it would be, but I always forgot how the air felt thick when it went into my lungs.

"Hey, Sammy!" my uncle called across the baggage claim in his pseudo-Southern accent. I waved in response, feeling awkward about yelling across a half-empty terminal in Indianapolis.

"Hi, Uncle Steve," I let out when I got closer and he picked me up. A very tiny human looked at me judgmentally. "And I assume you are Belinda?" The tiny human nodded, still judging me with her big brown eyes.

"Beli, say hi to your cousin."

"Hi, cousin."

"Sammy."

"Sammy," she repeated dutifully.

"It's Sam, actually. And Uncle Steve? I insist that you stop calling your four-year-old 'belly.' It's absolutely going to ruin the rest of her life."

"Hardy-har-har. Such big city attitude. We need to get you up on a tractor."

"I am strictly here in an office-managing-phone-answering capacity. There will be no tractor."

"Yeah, yeah," my uncle replied, picking Belinda up and swinging her over his massive shoulders. I settled in for the two-hour ride to the countryside, and I was sincerely hoping I got all of the crying done in St. Louis.

———

"How long has it been since you been here?" my uncle asked.

"Ummmm, five years?"

"Do you remember my friend Randy's son, Blake?"

"Vaguely... something with a soapbox building adventure is coming to mind."

"That's the one. He said he'd come 'round tonight and take you out."

"I'm sorry, what? Why?"

"They was out helping me unload beams from the trailer and I mentioned you'd be here and didn't know anyone."

"You scheduled me a playdate?"

"What's a playdate?"

"I'm seventeen. You can't just find someone my age and then make us go out together. This is going to be horribly awkward and you have to call and cancel immediately."

"I most certainly will not. He's bein' polite, and there's nothin' to be awkward about it."

I stared at him, trying to jedi-mind-trick him into agreeing with me, but he wasn't bothered by it. "Fine, whatever. I'll go on my weird playdate." I considered the fact that even if it was horribly awkward, it beat sitting around on my phone and pathetically waiting for snaps of Chris and ho-of-the-week to show up. "Do I need to, like, dress like a farmer?"

"I believe that is the required dress code for anywhere in town. Hope you brought your overalls, sassy pants." I just laughed and changed the radio station to something he'd roll his eyes at.

———

I had on a pair of Chucks, a black t-shirt, and jeans, and while I debated about straightening my hair, it stayed in the messiest of buns. I could not live down trying too hard on my arranged date. The bell rang, and I resigned myself to my fate.

"I'm going!" I called to my uncle.

"Be home by eleven!" he called back. I couldn't imagine staying out past eleven making small talk. I swung open the screen door and found a surprisingly decent-looking member of the male species.

"Hello...." I offered, already regretting the messiest of buns.

"Hello to you. Sam, if I remember correctly?"

"That's me. Blake, right?"

The one and only." He grinned, and all I could think of was that he kind of looked like Archie. Less hot than the TV version, but hotter than the comic book version. Auburn hair, and a smirk that looked well-worn on his face.

"I literally know seven Blakes in my senior class."

"Wow. Way to bruise my ego early."

I honestly had no idea if he was flirting. "Well, would it make you feel better if I put you as the number one Blake on my list?" I decided I'd flirt back, just in case.

"I think it would."   He raised his eyebrows and turned towards his truck. It was a giant truck. Like a massive, I-needed-a-step-ladder-to-get-into-it truck.

"Wow. Don't you think this is a little understated?"

"Huh?"

"Nothing. I was kidding. It's a large truck." *Not big on the irony, then.*

"Here," he said, holding out his hand to help me catapult into the vehicle.

"Uh, thanks."

He loped around to the other side and leapt in. "You good with pizza?"

"Always."

"You good with a party?"

"Depends on the kind of party."

"Barn party. Out at my buddy's. There'll be music and beer."

"Do you typically drink and drive when you take a girl out for the first time?" My friend Claire had ended up with two broken ribs, a punctured lung, and a broken arm two years ago from an asshole driving home drunk. I wasn't a fan.

"Honestly? Yeah. But whatever, we don't have to party. I did tell my buddy I'd swing by, though. Or I could take you back home after dinner."

"We can go, that's fine. I can always drive us back. Or get an Uber or something." He snorted. "What's funny?"

"There are no Ubers here. Where do you think you are, girl?" He slapped my knee playfully. "But don't worry about it. I won't drink. Scout's Honor." I side-eyed him, but I felt better.

"So. Number One Blake. What do you do for fun?"

"Football. Girls. Truck. Beer. I'm a very easy man to please. How about yourself?" *Oh lord. You've landed yourself with the quintessential small-town hero.* I couldn't even be judgmental — this was exactly what I'd asked for. I decided I could either be the stuck-up princess he was thinking I was, or I could be whomever I wanted. No one knew me— not really, and I could be anyone. That sounded far more entertaining.

"Cheerleading. Guys. My Mustang. Wine Coolers." Other than Chris being a guy, zero of those things were true. If I ever did drink, it was cheap vodka. I was in the photography club and had never done a cheer in my life. And I drove a Nissan.

"A cheerleader, huh?" *That was a little bit too easy.*

"Yep. I do love to show my school spirit."

"I bet you do."

Total honesty? I knew then that this guy was a douche. But there was the thing about having someone pay attention to me in that way after replaying that stupid video of Chris over and over again that made me not care.

———

The Pizza Hut buffet was one of the town's main attractions, so it was not surprising that we ran into seventeen people that was "bros" with and had to talk to. Everyone asked me about California and if I could surf. I couldn't, but I said I could.

One very special individual, also named Sam, gave me his number and told me to call him if Blake didn't show me a good enough time. And no one thought this was weird. I was beginning to wonder if people from California should have to get a passport before coming here.

"So, Sam. What are you going to do here all summer?" Blake asked once his friends had headed off to the party.

"I'm not totally sure. I'll work in the office. Watch Belinda. I'm assuming there will be a lot of Netflix binging."

"Well, if you need any help with the Netflix and chill part, feel free to hit me up."

"Thanks so much for your generosity, Blake." He legitimately winked at me at that point, and I was glad we were going to a party. There might be someone else there I could talk to for entertainment.

"You ready to head out?"

"I think so. Thanks for dinner, it's been a long time since I've eaten at The Hut."

"No problem. Let's go get our drink on." I shot him a pointed look.

"Let's go get *your* drink on. Wine coolers for you and soda for me." He flung his arm around my shoulders on our way back to the truck and helped me back into the passenger seat.

"Is this party in an actual barn?"

"Uh, yeah. That's the idea of a barn party."

"Got it. Let's do it, then."

"It's sort of hot when you say that." He replied as he started the truck. It was a very different world I was in, being hit on that overtly. He didn't seem to require a response, so I didn't give one.

I checked my phone on the way over and saw a snap on Chris' account. Why I continued to follow him was beyond me, but it almost felt like not knowing was worse than knowing. Until I actually checked the photo. It was a super classy selfie featuring three giant hickies on his neck. The text he'd added said "freedom".

My stomach did the rebellion thing, and tears pricked at my eyes at the stupidity of all of it. I was suddenly not at all put off by Blake's comments anymore.

———

"Raspberry or Strawberry?" Blake called from across the barn, holding up two wine coolers. He hadn't lied. It was a barn. With hay. And there was music, and there was beer.

"Both," I called back. No, it wasn't a good idea to drink two wine coolers. Or the three more I had after that. And yet, I did it anyway. To Blake's credit, even though there was a steady stream of very attractive girls who tried to pull him onto the "dance floor," he remained attentive. His breath in my ear felt nice after two drinks. His tongue in my ear felt really nice after five.

"Sit on my lap, California girl." I obliged, and let him run his hands up my T-shirt and under my bra. Other than Chris, I hadn't really had any experience with many guys. Maybe making out on a "date" freshman year, but nothing serious. My head was spinning, but still in a way that made me feel like I was having fun.

"Wanna know something?" Blake asked.

"Sure."

"The bed of my truck has all kinds of blankets in it. You know, if you're cold. We could go and warm up." I almost snorted at his transparency, but the three hickies kept flashing in my vision, and a very petty part of me wanted three of my own. Maybe not literally, because eww. But I needed someone else to want me. I giggled in the way one only does when drunk on wine coolers.

"Blankets sound delight. Delightful." Blake picked me up and threw me over his shoulder. I decided he had an okay ass while I was looking at it. He set me down lightly when we got to the truck and helped me hike into the truck bed. Sure enough, there were blankets aplenty which made the sober-ish section of my mind wonder about Blake's habits. He laid down and patted the spot next to him, and I appreciated his broad shoulders for the first time. He made sort of a comfy pillow. There was no more talking.

Blake leaned in and pushed his tongue into my mouth, moving his hands right back to where they were under my shirt, already unhooking my bra. *Don't overthink it, don't overthink it. Everybody hooks up.*

He took my hand and moved it to his belt, and I assumed he wanted me to undo it. I did and reached inside and gave him what I thought he was looking for. He slid his hand down the front of my jeans and under my white cotton underwear. I reached for his arm— it was too much.

"What's up, babe?" he asked.

"I don't know... just... I don't know." My head was fuzzy. And I had told him I wanted to go to his truck, and it wasn't like he was trying to have sex with me.

"Just let me make you feel good," he murmured in my ear as he slid his hand back under my pants. I let him kiss me again and tried to relax and let it feel good. Except it was about as enjoyable as having two carrots in my pants.

"I bet you give such good head." He pushed on my shoulders lightly to move me towards his zipper. *Just get it over with and go home.*

And I did.

My head was a lot less fuzzy afterward when he was telling me how hot I was. I felt all sorts of things, but hot wasn't one of them.

————

Blake didn't text me again, unless I counted the three a.m. "wanna meet up?" as communication, and I didn't. I was glad for it, though. I might have tried to convince myself that he was okay and gone out with him again, just so I could push back the vomitous feelings I had when I thought about that night. There would be zero more wine coolers. There would be zero more putting up with idiot guys who thought they were god's gift because they happened to be a big fish in a small pond. No more fish. No more pond. I was a Californian, and I'd be looking for someone who could swim the ocean with the sharks from now on.

Continued in The Summer of the Rabid Geese

What words would you use to describe this experience? Do you think the way this date ended is common or rare?

_____

_____

_____

_____

_____

What do you think Blake's perception was of Sam? Do you think Sam cares what his perception is?

_____

_____

_____

_____

_____

If you were Sam's friend, and she was telling you this story, what would be your response? Do you feel like this was an emotionally healthy experience?

_____

_____

_____

_____

_____

Did Blake do anything wrong? What do you think his response would have been if Sam had told him to take her home? Why?

_____

_____

_____

_____

_____

What can you take away from this story?

_____

_____

_____

ME, MYSELF? AND MANAIA

I knew when my Jordan's hit the pavement at the University of Miami (in Ohio...not Florida. I know, it's disappointing at first), that it was where I was supposed to be. There wasn't the constant tightness in my chest that I carried everywhere I went. It felt like a fresh start.

I still had the rest of senior year left, but my parents were big into having *plans* for their oldest kid. I walked through the nearest quad and tried to pick a word for how it felt. *Collegiate* was the only thing I could come up with, and that felt lame, but the whole thing— the columns, the brick, the burnt orange leaves and the chapel in the distance— it all felt like it was out of a movie. There were even students reading under trees.

The imposter syndrome was heavy as I tried to look like I knew what I was doing there. I'd hoped I'd see Kent's dorm right away without having to look at one of those map kiosk things, but it didn't work out. I traced my finger down the map until I saw Tappan Hall. *Got it.*

"You need directions somewhere?" a voice questioned from my left.

"Oh, I think I got—" I turned and saw the smiling face of a bronze-skinned Polynesian god staring back at me. "It. I think I got it."

His eyes danced when I tripped over my words. He was dressed in a white long-sleeved shirt and jeans, but I didn't think it really would have mattered if he'd been wearing a garbage bag.

"Okay, if you're sure." The god-man started to walk away, and something about being in that place where no one knew me… it had an effect.

"But, I mean, you can walk me if it would mean that much to you. Tappan Hall?"

The smile came out again, and he brushed his dark hair out of his face. "Easy enough. I live there. I'm Manaia, by the way." He said it like *man-eye-a*, and I already wanted him to say it again.

"Troy. Thanks for offering. I, uh, I'm just visiting a friend." He started walking out of the quad, and I fell in step beside him. He was taller than me… easily as tall as Luke. I made a conscious effort to push Luke from my head. We had reached a sort-of-stable place in our friendship, and I'd moved on. Kind of.

"Troy, got it. So, if you don't go here, where *do* you go?"

Really? He's gotta call out my age right off the bat? "Ah, I'm a senior. I'm thinking of coming here next year, so I'm visiting a buddy I used to play basketball with."

"Sweet. I used to play too— center. Are you tryina play college ball?" He didn't seem to care at all that I was still in high school.

"Cool. I play point guard. But I'm done after this season. Any wise words about why I should come to Miami?"

"Besides the obvious?" he asked, looking around as we passed more columned buildings and tree-lined paths.

"Besides the obvious."

"Well, I go here, so that's probably at least enough to tip the scales of most pro/con lists." He grinned again, and I could have sworn he was flirting with me.

"Oh, at least by ten. Maybe even five more since you might be able to take me one-on-one." As soon as the words came out of my mouth, I wanted to pull them back in. I honestly hadn't meant it to sound so... like I was drooling over him. I was, but that wasn't what I was trying to put out there. I felt heat spread over my cheeks and down between my shoulder blades. I needed *serious* practice on how to flirt with guys before I left for college. "In basketball. I meant. I mean. Basketball."

Manaia let out a genuine laugh. "Relax, Troy. That was kind of a badass line."

"I... um. Thanks." I wanted to die.

"We're here, by the way." I looked up and saw the large wrought iron letters that spelled out Tappan Hall.

"Awesome. Thanks." I was thanking him too much. I just wanted to get to Kent's room and never think about this again.

"Give me your phone," he said as I turned away. I took out my phone and handed it to him, hoping he couldn't see my hand shake. "I don't know how long you're here for, but text me if you wanna hang out. Or if you wanna see if I can take you one-on-one. However you meant it." He handed my phone back to me, smiled, and disappeared into the building.

Holy shit.

———

The stupid grin I had on my face lasted about three point two seconds before all of the self-doubt crashed down. *What if he was just joking? What if he* wasn't. *What if there's some god-awful hazing ritual these people do to gay freshmen?* I walked through the door of the dorm trying to push those thoughts back down and enjoy that I'd met a guy out in the wild. I'd been to some LGBTQ meet-ups in Cincinnati— that felt far enough away from Gem to be comfortable— but they always felt sort of structured. Like a play-date. I'd met one guy, and we'd hung out, but it never really went anywhere. *You are so far out of your league here.*

I let it go at that and told myself I wouldn't text him, even though I wanted to. I'd just hang out with Kent and see the campus and go home. *Maybe you could save his number for the fall, though... just in case.*

The inside of the building was surprisingly cozy. Leather chairs sat in the lobby, and it just didn't feel like what I'd pictured. I made my way up to the third floor where Kent said his room was. His door was open when I got to the number he'd given me, so I tentatively knocked on the wall before stepping inside.

"Aimes! Bro, welcome to my humble home," Kent greeted, hopping out of a folding chair. He held out his hand for an old Gem City High basketball handshake of sorts. Kent was the kind of guy everyone liked in high school. Brown hair, blue eyes, good-natured.

The dorm room was bigger than I thought it'd be. They had a tall mini-fridge, two beds, desks, dressers, and some extra chairs.

"Hey, man. It's been a long time. I like the room."

"Thanks. It's a little weird at first, *living* in the same room with another guy. But you get used to it after a few weeks. And there's a lot to do on campus, so I'm not here all that often." He grabbed another folding chair and handed it to me. My heart constricted in my chest about the thought of rooming with a guy as beautiful as Manaia. It would either be the best thing or worst thing that could possibly happen.

"Yeah… that seems like it could be, I don't know, different."

"So, what do you wanna do? Food? Go to the rec center and shoot some hoops? My girlfriend lives in Emerson next door, and her roommate's kind of hot— we can meet up with them for dinner if you want." Kent shrugged and went to rummage through his closet. He pulled out a hoodie and looked at me expectantly.

I realized I was going to have to keep playing the same role. I wasn't *out*. At least not to many people, and there was a very real chance Kent wouldn't want me to sleep in his room if I came out and told him I was gay, even though I'd never felt any attraction to him whatsoever. To a lot of guys, it didn't matter. I stood up and chewed the inside of my cheek.

"What's wrong, dude?" Kent looked genuinely concerned.

If I told him, it would probably be a well-known fact at GCH before I even got home. So I sighed and said, "Nothing. Food sounds good."

"It *is* good. You'll be pleasantly surprised." He clapped me on the back as we left his room.

I wasn't surprised. It was a disappointingly normal feeling for me to lie.

The food was delicious. Lasagna. And Kent's girlfriend was chatty and welcoming, and her roommate was, in fact, pretty. I'd felt so free when I stepped on campus, like this was a place I'd be able to be myself, but now I wasn't sure such a place existed. *Maybe you should just go home.*

"Well, now that we've carb-loaded, you wanna go jump in on a pick-up game?" Kent asked as the girls said goodbye and headed back towards their room.

"Uh, yeah, that sounds like a plan." I was pissed off that the only thing holding me back from really getting something out of this campus visit was *me*. Literally just me refusing to be honest. "Hey, do you care if I invite this guy I met earlier? His name's Manaia; he said he plays." I blurted it out quickly before I could change my mind.

"Manny? Hell yeah, that guy's awesome. Did you get his number, or do you wanna swing by his room?"

"I got his number." *Manny?* That did not do justice to the mythological status I'd given Manaia in my head.

. . .

T: Hey, this is Troy...from earlier today. My buddy Kent and I are going to the rec center. You wanna go?

M: I knew I'd be too much for you to resist texting ;). I'll meet you over there in 30.

That was a lot easier that I thought. "Okay, he's gonna meet us over there in like a half hour."

"Cool. You know he's gay? Killer ball player, though." We walked back into Tappan hall to get changed, and I almost choked on my own saliva.

"Oh... oh yeah? Cool." *Cool? And what the fuck does he mean he's a killer ball player,* though? *Like basketball skills have anything to do with—*

"You all right, man? You seem on edge," Kent commented as he unlocked the door to his room.

Whatever. Just fuck everything. "I'm gay, Kent," I muttered once we were safely inside his room.

"Shut up, man!" Kent laughed. Then the laughter died in his throat when he looked at my face. "Oh. Really? That's fine, I mean, I never thought... or, like, do people know?"

"No, not really. I mean a few people, yeah. But not everyone."

"Oh, well no worries about hearing it from me, that's, you know, your business." Kent had his basketball shorts in his hand, and now looked completely lost as to what he should do with them.

"I didn't mean to... I'm sorry, maybe I should have just... I don't know. I met Manaia earlier and we kind of hit it off, and I thought maybe college would be different, and I wouldn't have to... whatever. I'm sorry. I'll change in the bathroom." I grabbed my bag and got my ass into the bathroom in record time. *That was stupid. That was so, so stupid.* I was going to have to sleep in my car or get a hotel room. Kent was a nice guy, but his discomfort was all too clear. I shut the door to a stall and pulled on my basketball shorts and a t-shirt before texting my mom.

T: Hey, can I use the credit card to get a hotel room tonight?

M: What's wrong?

T: Nothing... I just don't think staying with Kent is going to work out. I really like the school, though.

M: Are you sure? I mean yes, you can use the card, just nothing too expensive.

T: I'm sure. Thanks, Mom. I'll see you tomorrow.

I breathed a sigh of relief that I'd only have to make it through playing a game or two, and then I could get out of there. I could even tell Kent he didn't have to go to the rec center. I tried to push down the wave of worry that he wouldn't keep his word and at least hold onto my secret until I graduated. It had worked out with Luke— he never said anything to anyone. Not even Vanessa, as far as I knew, but it didn't make it less terrifying. It was just a bridge I'd have to cross when I came to it. Or jump off it. *Shit.*

———

I held my breath and knocked on Kent's door. I'd considered just walking out, but I felt like that might be even more awkward.

"Hey, you ready to go?" Kent asked. He seemed overly cheerful. Or maybe I was overreacting.

"Yeah. Uh, you don't have to go, or like, I don't know. I can just go shoot some hoops and get a hotel."

"Aimes... I don't care that you're gay. Seriously." My eyes flew around the hallway to see who was around before I remembered this wasn't Gem City. "I mean, if you wanna get a hotel because you don't wanna sleep on my dorm floor, that's one thing, but I'm not fourteen. I don't think it's contagious, or something."

I had a mild passive-aggressive urge to cough on him just because, but I let it go. "Yeah, okay. I might get a room just to have a mattress, but we're good. Let's go."

To Kent's credit, or maybe to my own discredit, he was genuinely informative on our walk to the rec center. He was a business major, and that's what I wanted to go into, so he was doing a pretty decent job of selling Miami.

We walked through the entrance, and I got a guest pass. "This weight room is pretty sweet."

"Yeah, and there are always some sports medicine guys wanting to give advice, so take advantage of that and maybe put some muscle on your chicken arms."

"These are not chicken arms. They're just lean cuts of meat," I protested, still looking around. There were several half-court rooms set up, and I tried to ignore the heat returning to my face when I saw Manaia already practicing some layups in one of them. With another guy. A guy who happened to look like freaking Steph Curry.

"Oh cool, he brought JJ. We can play two on two." *Could have mentioned JJ when I was going on about him before.* Whatever. We'd play two on two and I'd go to the Comfort Inn I saw on my drive in. The irony of the name of the hotel was not lost on me.

"Hey, Troy, Kenny," Manaia called when we got through the glass door.

"Kenny, huh?" I smirked.

"Eh, payback for calling him Manny."

"You know it," Manaia replied. "This is my roommate, JJ. JJ, this is Troy, you know Kent." *Roommate. Not boyfriend.* I let that sink in and realized I hadn't said anything. Not at all awkward.

"Hey, nice to meet you. You guys down for two on two?"

"Yeah. I'll play with Troy," Manaia stated as if it were obvious.

"I'm hurt," Kent joked. "And sucks to be you because I'm better than Troy."

"Not even when I was a freshman, *Kenny*." I laughed and grabbed a quarter to toss. Manaia called it for heads in the air and we got first possession. I honestly didn't know how I could play when he was looking at me. I felt a little more aware of my chicken arms.

JJ didn't play quite as well as Steph Curry, but he was better than both Kent and me. Manaia was an all-out baller though. And not even a douche about it. I had a few high points in the game, but our win had very little to do with me. I was sweating like I was in the freaking Amazon, but so was Manaia, and I didn't totally hate that. I sucked down water and tried to towel off. This had not helped my crush situation at all, and I knew I was going to spend the night at a hotel wishing I were braver. JJ headed out shortly after, complaining that his girlfriend would kill him for showing up that sweaty. The word *girlfriend* had never brought me so much peace.

"So what are you guys up to tonight?" Manaia asked.

Kent looked at me as a question.

"Um, food? Then I'm gonna grab a hotel room and head home in the morning."

"Yes, Troy has decided he's too good to sleep on the floor."

"Man, when was the last time you cleaned your floor?" Manaia asked skeptically.

"I *clean*," Kent insisted.

"Yeah, no. I say, good call on the hotel room."

"See?" I affirmed. We headed out of the basketball court towards the showers, and my fingers jumped with nervous energy despite how spent I was.

"Well, I'm starving. Do you guys have something special planned, or is it cool if I invite myself to dinner?" Manaia asked, walking into the locker room.

My hands finally relaxed.

"I actually think I might meet up with Lexi, if that's cool, but you guys should go," Kent answered. Kent was officially the best wingman that ever lived. I tried to convey that with a look, but I wasn't totally sure it worked.

"Works for me. As long as you're not vegan. I need a burger, and that's kind of a deal breaker."

"Yeah, I mean, no, not a vegan."

"Cool. See ya, Kenny," Manaia called before heading to the showers.

"You're welcome," Kent said smugly.

"You're kind of a kickass wingman, Kenny," I told him.

"Yeah, you just watch it with the 'Kenny'."

"Thanks for today, though. Honestly. I think I wanna go here."

"Anytime, bro. Hit me up if you decide you do wanna crash." We put the GCH handshake to use again, and I grabbed a towel before the fastest shower known to man. I had a fear that Manaia would leave or think I left, or something else that was probably not going to happen, but I just needed to see him again as quickly as possible.

———

I didn't really pack anything to wear for a date. If this was even a date. But I threw on a faded red T-shirt and jeans and sufficiently messed up my hair. Manaia came up next to me in a Miami t-shirt and sweats, and *damn it*, he was still so hot. Like a cross between Bruno Mars and Jason Momoa hot. His black hair was wet and pulled back into a ponytail, and I had to bite my tongue to keep from saying something embarrassing.

"You ready?"

"Yeah, where did you have in mind? I have my car if you want me to drive."

"I was thinking Mac and Joe's— it's not far, we can walk. You can throw your bag in my room, or in your car, so you don't have to carry it."

"Good call."

"Did you pick up that I was preemptively inviting you back to my room after dinner?" His smile lit up his eyes, and I gripped the handle of my gym bag.

"I, uh, no, I didn't. Thanks for spelling it out though. Clearly I needed it." I laughed, but I was low key flipping out.

"Hey, sorry. I didn't mean it as, like, a given. You can put your stuff in your car, not a big deal."

"Is it that obvious that I have no idea what I'm doing?" I figured if I was failing miserably at playing it any kind of cool, I should just be honest and hope that worked.

"Only a little." He laughed. "I'm pretty much an open book though, so if you wanna say something or ask something, or whatever, you can." He slowed down as we came up to the Tappan Hall. "I'm gonna go throw my stuff in my room. You can come, you can wait here, it all works."

"I'll come with." I felt better with the honest approach. I followed him down a different hallway, and he unlocked the door to a room pretty much identical to Kent's, though this one was admittedly cleaner. And it had fewer posters.

"You need another water?" he asked, grabbing one from the fridge for himself.

"Yeah, sure." He looked at my bag before handing me the water, and I made a conscious decision to drop it before taking a drink. I was feeling somewhat braver after just owning up to my own inexperience. "Can I ask you something?"

"Sure." He dropped into his desk chair like he knew this might be a minute.

"How are things... here. I mean, being out? Sometimes, I think maybe I'm imagining college as some sort of safe haven, but really I get that nowhere is... I just... I want to be prepared, if I can be."

"I guess things aren't bad, you know? I mean, some people are still assholes, but people are gonna be assholes every- where. I try to make sure I'm not in a situation where I'm surrounded by people who may take their homophobia to the next level. Because that's always a worry, I can't lie about that. But I feel good here, as a general rule. I don't know if that helps or not."

"It does. I mean, I wish it could be better than that, but that sounds better than where I'm from."

"You ready to have a solidly above-average burger?" he asked.

"Let's do it."

———

It was a date. Like an actual date where he flirted and played with my fingers from across the table. And we talked about sports and the fact that he was pre-med and wanted to work on diabetes research... and it honestly blew my mind at how *easy* it felt.

The bill came, and I reached for it, but he was quicker. "I invited myself and scared Kenny away, I've got it," he insisted. I held up my hands in surrender and let him pay. That was a first. Even when I'd been hanging out with Kyle, we hadn't gone on a *date*. "You ready?"

"Yeah. You wanna watch a movie or something?" I didn't know what the protocol was. *Am I sleeping at his dorm? Will JJ be there?* My heart started racing when I thought about what he would expect, or even what *I* expected. I felt like my overall experience was three years behind because I was gay, and it sucked.

"Yeah, that sounds good." I obsessively started playing with the popsocket on my phone as we walked back. When we made it to his room, I thought my heart might come out of my chest. *Should I sit on the bed or the chair?*

"Troy?" Manaia asked, waving his hand in front of my face.

"Yeah? Sorry."

"Don't apologize. Just, are you okay? We can go to the common area and hang out if you want." His eyebrows knitted together in concern, and I just felt stupid.

"No, I'm fine."

"Ya sure? Again, open book." He sat down on his bed, leaning back against the wall.

"Um, I just... I haven't ever really hooked up."

"Okay, what does 'hooked up' mean?"

"Shit. This is incredibly awkward." I sat in his desk chair and faced him.

"It really doesn't have to be. I sort of learned the hard way that you have to be able to set boundaries. I get that there probably aren't a lot of other *out* guys in your town, and there weren't really for me, either. But that doesn't mean you have to do things you don't want to do because you met one gay guy. I mean, I'm awesome, but you get what I'm saying."

I did get what he was saying. I felt like if I did the wrong thing or didn't do the right thing, then he would disappear. "Okay. You're like a gay Yoda."

"I really am," he agreed, grinning.

"So I've, like, made out with a guy. And more with a girl, when I tried to convince myself I wasn't gay. But that's it."

"I've had one serious relationship that went on for two years," he said, "and one I thought was more serious than it was. Other than that, just casual, dating, whatever."

"Two years is a long time."

"It was. But I'm good with that being over now."

"That's... good," I breathed. Manaia leaned forward into my space, and I was drawn to the edge of the chair.

"I'm going to kiss you, if that's cool," he grinned. I pressed my lips to his first, and I liked the small shock wave I felt go through him before he kissed me back. My skin heated wherever his fingers traveled. I had just met him, but he knew more of the real me than most of the people I'd known my whole life.

We didn't ever get around to watching a movie, but how free I felt that night couldn't have been outshined even if I'd scripted it. For the first time in a really long time, I was me, and that was enough.

How did Manaia make things less awkward for Troy and discuss what each is *really* thinking?

_____

_____

_____

_____

_____

Why do conversations about boundaries and comfort levels seem uncomfortable for some and very easy for others? What's the difference in how they approach these topics?

_____

_____

_____

_____

_____

Do you think that Kent's reaction to Troy coming out is typical or not? What do you think causes other people to react differently?

_____

_____

_____

_____

_____

What can you take away from this story?

_____

_____

_____

_____

_____

Thoughts:

_____

_____

_____

_____

YOUR TURN: PERSONAL JOURNAL
SETTING BOUNDARIES

Make an honest list about where your boundaries lie. This isn't about what you think you *should* be comfortable with. This is between you and yourself so that you can learn to make these boundaries clear to others without feeling unsure because you've already done that work. And yes, boundaries change. With age, with time, within specific relationships, but the goal is to always make sure you're drawing your own lines— not following someone else's.

Physical Boundaries

Are you confident and comfortable holding hands, kissing, being touched, having sex? Think about this seriously— what things make you feel appreciated and excited, and what things make you feel nervous or afraid? This would include things like sending pictures or specific kinds of texts. (more information about the legal aspects of sexting provided by HealthForTeens.co.uk here: bit.ly/2AcMB0D)

. . .

Emotional Boundaries

Are you confident and comfortable seeing someone exclusively? Would you talk to them every day/night? How often would you see this person? How often would you spend time with your friends with or without this person?

From Here:

Are there changes you need to make in a current relationship?

_____

_____

(Are you overwhelmed? Have you agreed to something that you realize you're not comfortable with?)

_____

_____

_____

_____

_____

Are there things you need to speak to a parent, doctor, or other trusted adult about? (Like protection, birth control, sex-ed questions)

_____

_____

_____

_____

_____

Make a list of possible conversation topics you need to address and with whom. Also, note anything you're nervous about in having these conversations so that you can address those in the next section:

Ways to Have an Awkward Conversation

At this moment, you might be thinking that you'd like to put this book down and pretend it never existed (or not, you might be feeling empowered— go you!). But in the case of the former, let's look at some ways that you can address awkward conversations. Not all of these techniques are for every person. Specific ideas may speak to you based on whether you're an introvert/extrovert, your cultural background, and your relationship with your significant other or family. But, the good news is, they'll all work if you make the effort.

Rate each on a scale of 1-5, five being extremely comfortable for you, and 1 being so uncomfortable you would not consider it. Understand that you can't control someone's reaction to your boundaries, but you can work to explain yourself clearly. Also, do not apologize for setting boundaries. Ever. You are responsible to you and making sure you're taking care of yourself. While it may seem awkward, making sure you feel good in your relationships shouldn't be awkward at all.

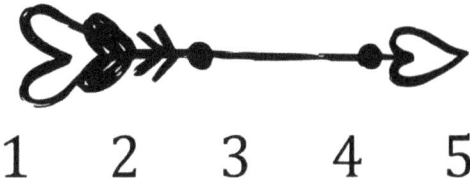

1 2 3 4 5

Technique & Explanation

Bold and To the Point

This technique is best if you're very comfortable asserting yourself verbally and you have a very open relationship with the person you plan on speaking to. This technique involves stating your intention and planning to have the conversation immediately. Examples:

"Mom/Dad, I'm thinking of having sex with _____ and I'd like to be safe about it and order some condoms/start on birth control. I also have some questions about some things I've heard from friends, so could we talk about those?"

"_____, we've been doing some things lately that I thought I was ready for, but I want to take a step back and stay where I'm comfortable. My feelings for you haven't changed. I just feel _____ when we _____, and I want to talk about it before it happens again.

RATING:

_____

Planned and Purposeful

This is a technique that might be better if you'd like

time for both you and the other person involved in the conversation to prepare. You might text the person and let them know you'd like to sit down to talk about one specific topic. You could choose a place where you're comfortable. It might also be helpful to bring this journal with you or a bullet point list of things you want to discuss. This may seem formal, but for some people, having a structure makes things less unpredictable and therefore less awkward.

Examples:
"Mom/Dad, I'd like to have a conversation about my relationship with _____. It feels like things are getting serious, and I want to talk about what that means. Could we sit down at dinner tomorrow night?"
"Hey, I know we've been joking around/hinting at where we'd like things to go between us physically. I'd like to actually talk about it to make sure we're on the same page. I don't want it to be awkward, I just think it's important that we know what's up... call me at ___?"

RATING:

———

Clear But Quiet
If the idea of having this conversation face to face isn't something you can think about right now, I might suggest a written version. Please be aware, however, that anything you write or text can be shared without your permission, so while this tech-

nique may feel "safer," there is something to be said for having a verbal conversation. This could be done over text or an actual written letter/journal to be passed back and forth. Again, I stress the fact that words without a voice/facial expression can be taken out of context, so, if you're okay with it, I would recommend doing this while in the same room together. That seems odd, but trading a piece of paper or journal back and forth allows you the time to read, process, and respond without the risk of having to wait an hour or longer for a response to what you wrote, or the risk of having someone else intercept your messages.

You could use any of the examples listed previously, but in a written format. The same structure applies — have a goal, be clear about what you want, and be open to accepting the other person's thoughts without being defensive.

RATING:

There is no rule that says you have to be ready for this level of conversation today. You may start with some basics- what your ideal relationship is, things you want to avoid, things you're fearful of, what kind of relationship you hope to have, or questions you have. You may just want to talk about the stories in this section— they're heavy. There is a lot of "stuff" there, so use it! It's still good practice to get comfortable with the important conversations. The more you have them, the less awkward they will be.

. . .

Make an outline for a conversation you think you may need to have. Feel free to use the stories in this section as the basis of your conversation if that's more comfortable than talking about your own experiences or experiences of friends. Always make sure you set ground rules before sharing any stories that are not your own. Will you change the names of people when you share their story? Is the person you're talking to comfortable hearing stories about others? This is why the short stories can be a good starting point.

Outline/Brainstorming:

_____

_____

_____

_____

_____

_____

_____

_____

_____

_____

But What If?

This section has really focused on how to determine boundaries and convey them to people in your life, hopefully people who care about you. But that isn't always the case. There is a very real (and unfortunate) probability that your boundaries will come into play in situations where you don't have the opportunity to have big conversations. Situations where someone is in your space and you haven't invited him or her there. Situations where you are with someone who wants something you aren't willing to give, and you either don't know how to tell them that, or they don't want to hear that. The section on Consent really comes back into play here, but we can't talk about boundaries without reviewing consent, so here we go.

This part is important:

YOU DON'T OWE ANYONE ANYTHING.

Not even if they were really nice to you, not even if they are more popular/experienced than you, not even if they are your very best friend in the whole world. Not even if you think you might make a scene or if you might hurt someone's feelings or if it's "not that big of a deal." It's not your job to allow something to happen to you that you don't want to happen just because it might be awkward for someone else. Go back to Emma's story and really think about where her head was in that situation. Think about the story with the guy who couldn't handle his girlfriend's manipulation. Why did he stay with her, why did he hesitate? Have a plan ahead of time if someone makes you uncomfortable. *And*— no matter what steps you take or don't take, no one has the right to touch you without your consent. Someone else's actions are never your fault.

. . .

Things you can do:

- Practice being direct and clear. Actually practice saying these things out loud. "This is not okay." "I'm really uncomfortable." "I'm going to go."
- If you're in a place with other people you know, find a group and take yourself out of that situation.
- Leave. Call an Uber, get in your car, call your parents. If possible, just leave if your gut tells you to leave. No explanation necessary. You can develop a code word for your parents if you don't want to make it sound like you're calling them to pick you up. It could be "Hey, what time is brunch tomorrow?" Then they know they need to be on their way.
- If a situation goes from uncomfortable to dangerous, you do whatever you need to do to protect yourself. Resources and information on this topic can be found at rainn.org

At the same time, be aware of how others react to you. You may know your intentions are harmless or flirtatious or innocent, but pay attention.

- Does the other person have his or her arms crossed?
- Does he or she lean into you or away from you?
- Is the other person smiling or laughing naturally?

- Are your touches or flirtations reciprocated?

The easiest way to know if someone else is feeling you is to *ask*.

- Are you cool with this?
- Is this okay?
- Can I kiss you?

Or honestly any variation of this. As you've been practicing your own boundaries and figuring yourself out, recognize that everyone else has their own comfort levels and things they're working on.

Rate your comfort level on reading body language and asking others for their boundaries.

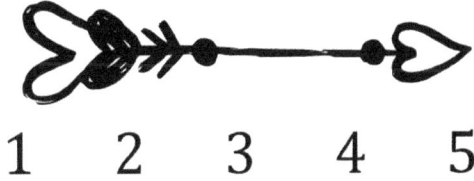

1   2   3   4   5

Thoughts, Concerns, or Fears: (Consider talking to someone you trust about these)

_____

_____

_____

_____

_____

_____

_____

_____

_____

_____

_____

_____

_____

_____

_____

_____

_____

_____

_____

_____

_____

_____

_____

_____

_____

_____

_____

_____

DRAWING THE LINE

Boys will be boys.

— SEEMS LIKE EVERYONE, EVERYWHERE

What does this even mean? Again, I say that this is offensive to both genders. So, males can't possibly control themselves? And females are supposed to be held to a higher standard? And they're supposed to forgive things because they were done by a boy? This is lazy. And completely stupid.

———

Drawing the line. This is a big deal. This is the point when all of the other work of figuring out your boundaries and the boundaries of others— it comes to the point where it's a yes or a no. This can be exhilarating. Or perhaps disappointing. And, in some cases, freaking scary. But either way, it's real.

There's no time limit on when you're able to draw your line. If you find yourself in a situation where this hasn't happened yet, and you feel like it needs to happen, then that's all there is. There is no more important conversation with someone you're involved with than the one that allows you to be heard. And I don't mean to make it sound like you need to have a legal pad and a clipboard. You could. Or you could just start with "Hey, here's where I'm at..." The important thing is that you can say what you need to say. And if you feel like you can't, then that's something else to think about entirely, and it's time to reach out to your support system.

This is your life, and you have a right to be honest about what you want out of a relationship, and so does everyone else. It hurts to walk away or to be walked away from, but this is part of the human complexity I mentioned earlier. The idea that two people are on the exact same page on every issue all the time is fantasy. Real life doesn't work that way, and it's important to practice speaking your mind rather than trying to find someone who can read it.

<3 Nicole

THE SUMMER OF THE RABID GEESE

There was something to be said for the humidity and the one-main-road and the single-screen movie theater in that town. Most of that something was made up of expletives, but there were a few redeeming qualities. Namely that my boyfriend – ex-boyfriend – was easily two thousand miles away.

I was sitting in the pick-up I'd borrowed from my uncle outside of Wal-Mart. Yes, it was a very picturesque scene. I was sitting and wondering if my previous decision to swear off all small-town-farm-boys was a mistake. Because I was *bored*. True to my word, I hadn't had a date at all except for the one regretful night with the cheap wine coolers and the guy with the way too lifted truck that was *absolutely* compensating for something. I was also sweating. And swearing internally because it was freaking hot, and there weren't enough hair products in the world to make my hair straight under these conditions. I tried my best with a wavy updo, but that didn't mean it was working.

Times were desperate. I was so in need of entertainment that I almost found myself wishing summer would come to an end so that I could go home and return to my life of little excitement in Nor Cal. I turned the air up again. I couldn't decide on the perfect temperature inside the vehicle. It was also possible that I was hyper-fixating on the temperature while secretly trying to decide if I was crazy enough to march into the Wal-Mart and make eye-contact with random members of the male gender until one of them felt compelled to ask me to dinner. I didn't even care if it was to Taco Bell; I needed to go out. Thanks to Snapchat, I knew Chris absolutely wasn't sitting around wishing for dates, because he had them. A lot of them.

I'd been there for weeks working for my uncle to pad my resume before college, but seeing my friends' adventures from break show up in my feed was making me feel like my decision was absolute shit. I refused to go home without my own tale to tell, and *not* the tale of me and *Blake*. That one was going to the grave with me. I happened to check my DMs while fighting back a wave of self-pity and jealousy, and saw a request sitting there from a name I vaguely recognized. *Ryan Trent.*

RyGuyBaconLover: Hey... this is Sam, right? The Samantha Riley whose pool I swam in when we were, like, twelve? Anyway, this is random, but my mom said she talked to your mom and that you're in town for the summer, and I'm on leave and wanted to see if you were down to visit one of the many attractions rural Illinois has to offer. And if this isn't Samantha Riley, well, shame on you for reading this far into a clearly personal message to an old friend ;).

. . .

My initial reaction was trying to recall a friend of my mom's from high school coming to visit us with her kids a good five or six years ago. The memory was there, and I didn't have any immediate horrible flashbacks, so that was positive. My second thought was that this person could very seriously be a serial killer who uses vague childhood memories to lure his victims. I ventured to his feed, which wasn't at all like cyber stalking, because he messaged me first; plus, it was clearly a necessity to make sure the memory was real to cut down on the murdering possibilities. I wanted a date, but not if it was going to be my last one.

The first photo on his feed was of him in an air force uniform with another guy who must have been in his squadron. *Squadron? Unit? Battalion?* I wasn't particularly up-to-date on my military lingo, but I was perfectly capable of turning into a cliché at the sight of cute boy in uniform. There was also a photo in the mix of him with his family, and his mom actually did look familiar, so I was growing more confident that this whole thing was exactly what a small-town summer adventure was supposed to be about— that and the lightning bugs and people who wave hello at you when you drive by them on the highway.

I pressed my mother's name in my phone book hastily, realizing I really either needed to go into Wal-Mart or turn off the car before I was the unfortunate soul who ran out of gas in the parking lot. I checked my makeup in the rearview while the phone rang, suddenly aware of the possibility in a town that small that my secret DM-er could magically show up at any moment. I looked like my face was melting, which was a pretty accurate description of how I felt after filing papers in a poorly ventilated storage closet all day.

"Hey sweetie, what's up?" she answered.

"Do you or do you not have a friend with the last name of Trent who lives near here?"

"Nice to hear from you, too. I miss your shining presence in our home."

"Mom. This is a matter of love or murder."

"I don't particularly miss your drama. But yes, I have a friend named Marilyn Trent who lives there. You've met her."

"And she has a son named Ryan."

"She does. I think he's in the military." That was a good enough answer to convince me that I would not be contacting an ax murderer, and it made me want to dance out of my seat.

"Thank you, mother, you've been *most* helpful. Love you!" She started to say something else, but that was obviously the end of the conversation.

Back to my DMs I went, to craft a somewhat-casual response, but let's be honest, I was bored out of my skull and in no place to play games.

Samanth.Ability: Ryan, of course, my long-lost childhood friend. I am in town for the summer working for my uncle. I'm game to get together, as long as wherever we go has other people under the age of fifty. I'd really like to say I have to check my calendar, but most of my major plans at the moment revolve around braving the rabid geese at the park with my cousin.

I included my cell number and hit 'send' before I could worry about coming across as desperate, and I forced myself to get out of the car to hunt for a new shirt that could either say *I don't particularly care if you like me* or *I heart Air Force men*. I expected a lot out of Wal-Mart. I also made a mental note to look for some more lying hair products that claimed to fight humidity.

———

I may have checked my phone every fifteen minutes –*seconds*-, but I didn't have to wait long. I was in a startlingly clean dressing room stretching a purple halter-top over my head when my phone rang. When I saw the local number, I almost didn't answer. I didn't know what kind of person called rather than texted, and I didn't even know if I remembered how to speak to a guy on the phone. I then took a look around and remembered my small-town-adventure motto.

"Hello?"

"Hey... is this Samantha?"

"It is, is this Ryan?"

"Sorry for calling. I was driving when I got your message."

"Oh, no worries. Very responsible not to text and drive, I get it. And call me Sam." *Why did people ever enjoy talking on the phone? This is awful.*

"Cool. So, Sam. What are you doing?"

"Ummmm."

"Oh god, you're not, like, in the bathroom or something, are you?"

"No! No. I'm in a dressing room. I... well, I am doing what one does in a dressing room."

Ryan started laughing out loud. "That is a much better image than the other. But sorry again. I'm not really killing it with this second first impression, am I?"

"No, actually, this is intensely awkward. But I suppose it can only go up from here." That fact that he was already flirting with me after not having seen me for six years made me consider that something was wrong with him. *Is this not exactly what you wanted? Cute boy...flirtatious manner... summer fling?*

"I like your optimism. At the risk of sounding like I'm trying to avoid small talk, which I'm totally not because I love small talk, when are you free?"

"That's not a polite question, Ryan. You now put me in the position of sounding too eager or uninterested. Try again." I was smiling even as I sat with half a halter-top on and the phone pressed to my ear to drown out the din outside the door. That had to be at least a semi-good sign.

"Forgive me, I strive to be nothing if not polite. Are you free tonight?" I could feel him smiling back. He had a good voice— it wasn't too deep, but it sounded happy, like there was a laugh constantly riding behind it.

"As it happens, I am."

"Would you do me the great honor of accompanying me to dinner? No senior citizen specials, I swear."

"Okay, now maybe too polite."

"You're very specific." *Shit, okay. Maybe turn it down a notch.*

"Sorry, I was just kidding. Dinner sounds good."

"So was I. We really aren't getting better at the awkwardness."

I breathed out. He was right, and I had to hope our conversation flowed a bit better in person.

"I'm still sticking with the optimism."

"I like it. Text me your uncle's address and I'll pick you up at six?"

"Yeah, that works. Thanks for messaging me."

"Thanks for messaging back and not thinking I was a serial killer."

"Well, while we're on the subject— are you a serial killer?"

"It was a career option, but they frown on it in the Air Force... something about protecting civilians, I don't totally get it."

"Well, thank goodness for the Air Force, then."

"I'll see you tonight."

"See you then." I hung up and breathed out a sigh of surprise. I didn't expect to feel nerves. I just wanted to get out of the house and put on makeup that wasn't done by my cousin for dress-up. But he had an actual sense of humor.

And I didn't feel the need to get off the phone right away... I could have kept talking to him.

I finally tossed the phone in my bag and looked in the mirror at my crazy self with one arm through the top. I smiled anyway, because I had a date.

———

I shook out my hair upside down as directed by my new product, and by the time I was done, it at least looked tame, falling in long brown waves past my shoulders. I'd ended up with an off-the-shoulder yellow top and jeans, because people seemed to only ever wear jeans there, but I stubbornly put on a pair of high black wedges that matched my bag.

"And where are you going, all fancied-up?" my Uncle Steve asked.

"Date." I shrugged like it was an every-night occurrence, but we all knew it wasn't— even my four-year-old cousin looked incredulous.

"Are you allowed to go on dates?"

My eyes rolled to the side. "I'm eighteen. Yes, I'm allowed to go on dates. *You* set me up on one not two weeks ago. And this one was even approved by my mother."

"Do you want me to get my shotgun out and set it by the door for when he gets here?" My uncle was not a kidder.

"I think it's okay to not. Like, do not do that. If it makes you feel better, though, I'll make sure he knows you *have* the shotgun."

"I have twenty-two shotguns."

"Okay. Twenty-two shotguns."

"Good. Well, you look pretty," he added as he turned back to his daughter in her high chair.

"Thanks, Uncle Steve." At that, I heard a car crunch down the gravel driveway and my posture inadvertently straightened. I peeked out the kitchen window and saw that he was driving a Volvo and not a truck, so Ryan already had one point in his favor after the debacle with guy-who-shall-now-remain-nameless. Thinking about that night still gave me the heebs. I let the blinds fall closed lest Ryan see me spying.

The bell rang, and I stood.

"Uh, are you gonna get that?"

"Shhh! Yes. I just need him to wait a second so it's not like I'm running to the door."

"Women are crazy," my uncle retorted. I supposed he was allowed to say that after my aunt up and left to be an aspiring country star six months before. I made my way to the door and opened it to find Ryan— who was much taller than I remembered— wearing a Modest Mouse T-shirt and a cowboy hat. Like, an honest-to-god cowboy hat made of what looked like straw, and I had no idea what my face looked like.

"Hey there, little lady," he drawled. He held the façade for all of five seconds before he busted out a smile of beautiful white teeth. "Okay, I was really going to try to keep that up for at least a minute, but you look horrified and now I feel bad." He laughed. He took off the hat, and he had perfectly normal, dirty blond hair underneath.

I smacked him in the arm. Kind of hard.

"Not funny, Ryan."

"Ow. And it was a little funny, *Sam*."

"You don't have to say my name like an insult. It's just my name."

He grinned again, and I had the urge to ask him where he got his dental work done— no way he just had teeth like that naturally.

"Okay, I won't say your name like an insult, and you promise next time I do something stupid, you don't hold back when you hit me."

"I agree to your terms."

"Then I think we're ready to go to dinner." I walked cautiously across the gravel in my heels and only flushed a little when he opened my door and I felt his hand on my back. I couldn't quite decide if the polite thing was for real or not, but I was trying to roll with it. I'd been with my last boyfriend for two years, and we were the "honk outside and wait in the car" kind of couple. The thoughts of Chris crept up the back of my brain, and I had to shove them away. Half the reason I was there was to clear my head about him— it would do no good to start a comparison this early.

"I'm sorry I hit you," I said hastily, and much too late, as I slid into the passenger seat.

"It's okay. I've never started a date that way before, so this is already something new."

"Sadly... I have started a date that way before. Sorry to disappoint."

"I don't think you're disappointing at all." He smiled at me again and shut my door. *Okay then, Ryan Trent. I'm intrigued.*

———

"So, how do you feel about Vietnamese food?" he asked once we were officially moving.

"Out in the real world? Fine. Here? I don't trust it."

He chuckled at that. "Yeah, me neither. I'd be down for some pretend Mexican food, though, if that's cool. I hear the owner has actually been to Mexico once, so it's gotta be authentic."

"Oh, for sure. Practically like getting street tacos in Mexico City. I'm game."

"Awesome," he agreed, turning onto *the* main road. The Volvo was nice, though I suspected it wasn't his— it didn't seem like a car someone would keep on a military base.

"So, where are you stationed?"

"I just finished basic in San Antonio, and I'll go back next week for technical training before finding out where I'll be stationed."

"Do you like it?" I personally couldn't imagine choosing to go through any kind of military training, but my grandpa had been an army ranger, so I knew a little bit from listening to his stories.

He squinted and hesitated. "I don't know yet."

"Oh?" I wasn't sure where to go with that.

"Sometimes I wake up wondering what in the hell I've done," he laughed. "But most of the guys are cool, and I got super ripped at basic." He totally gave me a side smirk while I inadvertently checked out his arms. He was kind of toned. But it annoyed me that he knew it.

"And you're clearly super humble too."

He laughed again. It was a good sound. He asked me about senior year, and I tried to make it sound exciting. He listened like he might actually remember some of it later. A whole ten minutes and one Podunk town over, we came to the Mexican restaurant, complete with a flag and brightly colored lights on the patio.

"Tell me more about these rabid geese," he implored as we sat down at an outside table.

"Why would I tell you when I could show you? As far as I'm aware, the park is open past sunset." He raised an eyebrow.

"You're totally in like with me right now, aren't you?" He grinned. "Trying to extend our date past dinner." He clucked his tongue at me and opened his menu.

"You're a little bit of an ass," I let him know as I opened mine as well.

"Yeah, I get that." He laughed. "If it makes you feel any better, I'm totally down to go for a sunset geese-watching walk with you at the park. I might even push you on the swings if you play your cards right."

It was one of those nights that sort of belonged in a scrap-book. I made him go and get the cowboy hat from his car for a brief photo shoot in our booth at the restaurant— because despite my initial horror, he kind of looked adorable in it.

True to his word, he did walk with me at the park, and he even grabbed my hand shortly after we started on the black-top. It didn't feel weird or forced or fake. I didn't actually notice it at first because it just seemed sort of normal. The geese, however, made a liar out of me because they were apparently sleeping, or nesting, or whatever the hell geese did at night.

"Sam... I have to tell you something," Ryan began.

"Oh god, what?" He was probably gay or engaged or something, because I found myself *liking* him.

"I think you were lying about the geese just to get me alone in the dark. I feel a little taken advantage of."

"Dammit— how did you figure out my goose façade? It *always* works. You, my friend, are too smart for your own good."

"Yeah, it's a curse." He squeezed my hand tighter at that point as we finished our walk around the lake.

"So. Sam. Anyplace else you want to lure me to?"

"My uncle has a hot tub," I blurted out, definitely not ready for the night to end yet.

"A hot tub, you say?"

"I did say."

"I don't know that I have trunks with me." He traced circle on my palm while he spoke, making my stomach do awkward things.

"I'm pretty sure boxers cover about the same area." I *sincerely* hoped my uncle was watching a fight or a NASCAR race on TV and hadn't decided to take an evening soak.

"Then yeah, I'm down. That sounds good, actually."

———

"Would you come here already?" Ryan asked after we'd been sitting on opposite sides of the spa for a good ten minutes talking about the difference between a small town and a city. I was having a hard time deciding how to act. I'd forgotten that I could be anyone— I'd just been myself all night, and that kind of freaked me out. That, and Ryan without a shirt was an experience in and of itself. I *had* said I wanted someone who could swim with the sharks... and he was in the fucking Air Force, so I was gonna go with 'yeah'. *Flying sharks, even.*

"Where?"

"Here," he answered, leaning forward and grabbing my hands so he could pull me over to him. I sat on his lap, and it didn't feel awkward. He held onto my hands and pressed on various pressure points under the water.

"That feels good," I let out, never having had anyone give me a hand massage before.

"Good," he murmured. We sat for a long time in the bubbles, and I relaxed into him, laying my head on his shoulder. Eventually he dropped my hands and wrapped his arms around my waist.

"I like this thing you call a swim suit," he said in my ear. I was glad it was dark, because I knew there was color spreading across my cheeks. I'd wavered between my black one-piece or the hot pink bikini one of my friends had talked me into buying back home. I'd gone with the pink one, and I wasn't the slightest bit sorry.

"I'm turning kind of pruny," I said, without really responding to him, holding out my hands.

"Is it cool if I come in and get changed? Or would your uncle not be okay…"

"Well, I'm sort of sitting on your lap while you're in your underwear, so I think we're past the point of worrying about my uncle would think. I hope."

He laughed again.

"Plus, I'm staying in the pool house."

"Your uncle has a pool house? I'm disappointed. That's not redneck at all."

"I know. Totally ruins the ambience, doesn't it?"

"I'll have to pretend it's a workshop or an old barn or something to make it better." He wrapped his arms around me after we got our towels and rested his chin on my shoulder as we walked along the paver stones to the pool house.

"There's a bathroom there, if you wanna change."

He'd thrown his clothes over his shoulder for the walk back, and I didn't totally want him to put them back on.

"What are these?" he asked, tilting his head towards the photos on the wall.

"I believe those are mostly family reunion photos from six or seven years ago. Notice the perm," I stated, referencing a picture of myself at age eleven. "I was clearly in a cute stage."

"I would say you're still in a cute stage," he responded lightly as he stepped in closer.

"Oh, would you, now?" I turned around to face him, still shivering in my towel, when he pressed his lips to mine. My lips parted and he deepened the kiss. His fingertips danced across my stomach and up my back, making me shiver even more, goose bumps breaking out across my skin. I stepped closer to him and let my hands rest on his hips, and I kissed him back, all thoughts of quippy remarks now lost.

I'd known the kiss was there all day, hanging between us, but I was almost glad he'd waited until then, when we were really alone, to make it happen, because I didn't want it to stop. There was something there with him. I felt my back hit the wall, and I let my fingers travel up to the back of his neck to pull him closer, but he pulled away.

"Is this... is this okay? Should I have asked before I kissed you? Are you cold?" He seemed nervous, and that made me feel a bit less nervous.

"This is definitely okay. And I'm less cold now than I was, but there are blankets... you know, in other places in this room."

"Ah, show me one of these places you speak of." His smile returned and he grabbed both of my hands before kissing me again. I led him to the open space that was acting as my room, or at least my room for the summer, and stopped at the pull-out couch.

"Sooooo. There are blankets here." I tilted my chin towards the pulled-out sofa that I hadn't bothered to make that morning.

"That there are," he confirmed, running his free hand through his hair.

"Do you want some water? Or I think there's soda in the mini fridge? Or..." *God, this is ruining all the moments.* I shifted my weight from one foot to the other, wishing he'd just kiss me again and we could skip the weird "should we or shouldn't we" conversation.

"Hey..."

"Yeah?"

"This doesn't have to be weird, does it?"

"Ummmmm, well? It's kind of weird right now, and I don't know how to make it unweird." I wasn't shy, and I *wanted* him in the worst way, but I hadn't ever gone there with a guy who wasn't Chris. He leaned down to brush my lips with his, and I held my breath, waiting for what he was going to say.

"I like you," he stated plainly.

"I like you, too."

"I would like to explore the area with the blankets."

I laughed at that.

"I would too."

"See how well this is going?" I nodded expectantly. He paused for a longer moment.

"Do we need condoms?" He asked this in the same tone as everything else, and the look on his face let me know that he was genuinely asking to be prepared, not to put pressure on us.

"Yeah. Yes, I mean. We do. Do you have some?" I tried to match his conversational manner.

"Yeah. Let me run out to my car— go ahead and get warm. I'll be right back." He kissed me again, with more heat this time, and then headed for the door.

I sort of forgot I was still damp and cold for a moment, but I finally made it to the closet and pulled out a soft hoodie and leggings. There was the question of why I was getting dressed when I just told him I wanted to have sex, but I felt like *me* wearing those clothes, and so they stayed. I sat on the edge of the bed and smiled to myself, having a hard time believing that something so random could have turned into something... well, something else entirely. I felt like I had known him a long time, and while that was kind of true in a weird way, it wasn't like we *knew* each other all these years.

Ryan stepped back into my room, and after meeting my eyes, was back where he left off, his lips on my skin and my hands on his bare chest. He kissed me in places only my ex had before, but instead of bringing back those memories, it felt like he was recording over them with new ones. When his still-wet boxers were on the floor and my hoodie and leggings long forgotten, I felt him hesitate.

"Are you sure you want to do this? I mean, I'm fine if this is all we do, or if you want more..."

"I want more," I told him definitively.

"Me too," he answered.

———

To be fair, he did say he needed to leave at least six times, but I wasn't totally ready for that. We made good use of his stash of latex, and the awkwardness of earlier was long forgotten.

"You might be a bad influence on me," he said into my shoulder.

"You can't honestly expect me to believe that you have national security clearance and shoot off military weapons on a daily basis but are worried about a curfew."

"You're right, I don't really expect you to believe it. This is way worth a worried mom text anyway." He kissed his way up to my neck again, and I let out a happy sigh.

"Walk me to my car?"

"Fine, fine." I finally gave in, knowing it was almost two a.m., and I actually did have to get up in the morning. I found my hoodie and leggings and regretfully watched Ryan get dressed too.

"Tonight was sort of awesome." He leaned against his car and pulled me closer.

"It *was* sort of awesome."

He bit his lip and looked worried, which wasn't an expression I'd seen him wear all night.

"What?"

"Nothing."

"Oh come on, tell me."

"It's kind of... I don't know, embarrassing, maybe? I hadn't planned on telling you if things went this way."

"Well, now you're kind of making me nervous, so spill it." I stepped back from him, worried that he had a girlfriend, and this had all been a giant mistake.

"No, no. Just... that was the first time... or first three times, I've ever done that." It dawned on me what he was saying, and I looked up, confused.

"Wait, seriously?"

"Seriously."

"I... I'm sorry?"

He genuinely laughed out loud at that. "Why would you be sorry?"

"I don't know. I could have lit a candle or something? I didn't know. Was, um... was this like a 'before I get shipped overseas I have to ditch my virginity' sort of task?" I felt a cloud settle over the night.

"No! No, Sam, I swear that wasn't it. I just really like you. I swear."

"Okay. Even if that's a lie, thanks for saying it."

"I'm sorry I said anything. I feel like I ruined it. Can I see you again before I go back to Texas?"

"Wow, booty call already, huh? You are a fast learner." I smiled when I said it, but it didn't really feel like a joke.

"Sam. I don't care if we go chase geese at the park. I was just trying to tell you that this meant something to me. Not to make you feel… whatever you're clearly feeling." He rubbed my arms with his hands, and it felt so good that I needed to believe him.

"Do you mean that?"

"I do. This whole night wasn't something I expected."

"Me neither."

"So is that a yes that I can see you?"

"That's a yes."

"Is it weird that I'm already thinking about how I can convince you to come visit me on base when I find out where I'm going?"

"Definitely weird. Kind of stalker-ish. But I like it."

"If that's what floats your boat, I'll keep it up."

"Hey, Ryan?"

"Hey, Sam."

"I'm really glad you were brave enough to hunt for the psychotic geese with me."

"I will protect you from rabies-infected geese anytime, Samantha Riley." He kissed me again before slipping into the driver's seat, and as my heart raced, I decided getting away for the summer was the best decision I ever made.
 Samantha Riley— Apparent Air Force Groupie, Goose Hunter, and Paper Filing Badass.

Whether or not you agree with Sam's choices, compare this encounter with Sam's first date of the summer. Why are things different?

_____

_____

_____

_____

_____

How did Ryan and Sam understand that there was consent throughout this experience?

_____

_____

_____

_____

_____

How does Sam decide what she wants and make it clear, or "draw the line"?

_____

_____

_____

_____

_____

How has Sam's outlook changed since *Big Fish, Small Pond*?

What can you take away from this story?

_____

_____

_____

_____

_____

Thoughts:

_____

_____

_____

_____

_____

_____

_____

_____

_____

_____

_____

_____

_____

_____

_____

_____

_____

_____

YOUR TURN: PERSONAL JOURNAL
SETTING BOUNDARIES

Young adults are notoriously pegged as impulsive. Part of this is fair because the pre-frontal cortex isn't fully developed until your early 20s, and this is the part of the brain that thinks things through, aka forethought. However, this doesn't mean young adults aren't capable of thinking things through— it just takes work.

The sections leading up to this have been all about forethought. Ideals, fears, hopes, concerns... all of this was the work you needed to do to lead to making decisions. And let me be clear in that those sections will need to be revisited. New stages in life, new relationships, etc. Things change. But now let's move into your real life. Where are you right now, and where do you want to go? How will you get there? Have you had the difficult conversations from the previous sections, and what effect have they had?

Here, you will revisit some of your previous thoughts, but rather than brainstorming, you'll be writing your own personal vision. Get ready, this is a big one! :)

If you're not currently in a relationship, begin here:

Think about the following and answer honestly:

Are you looking for a relationship?	☐Yes, casual ☐Yes, serious ☐No, not really ☐No, not at all	Reasoning:
How have your past relationships affected you? Lack thereof?		
In a perfect world, what would your relationship look like?		
In reality, what are things that are not acceptable, i.e. deal-breakers?		
What are your feelings/concerns about sex? Oral sex? Kissing?		

———

If you ARE in a relationship (casual or serious), begin here:

Think about the following and answer honestly:

Are you content and comfortable in where your relationship stands?	☐Yes, absolutely ☐Yes, mostly ☐No, not really ☐No, not at all	Reasoning:
If you answered anything but "yes, absolutely," what would need to change to get you there?		
Are these changes things that are under your control, or are you trying to change your partner? Does your partner want to change?		
If you did answer "yes, absolutely," where do you see things going in a month, six months, a year? Do you have any concerns?		
What are your feelings/concerns about sex? Oral sex? Kissing?		

10 Important Questions to Ask Yourself
In or Out of a Relationship:

Do I like myself? Or What do I like about myself?

_____

_____

_____

_____

_____

Would I be okay if a relationship ended? (if not, think about why, and ask yourself if your feelings are healthy.)

_____

_____

_____

_____

_____

Who makes up my support system outside of a relationship?

_____

_____

_____

_____

_____

Do I feel comfortable and confident expressing my boundaries, or do I need more practice?

_____

_____

_____

_____

_____

Do I have a clear sentence or phrase to express myself if I am uncomfortable or do not consent to something, or do I need to work on this?

_____

_____

_____

_____

_____

What are my personal goals outside of a relationship?

_____

_____

_____

_____

_____

Am I okay being alone with myself? Why or why not?

_____

_____

_____

_____

_____

Do I surround myself with people who support me?

_____

_____

_____

_____

_____

Do I have hobbies, friends, and interests outside of a rela-
tionship/potential relationship?

_____

_____

_____

_____

_____

Do I have somewhere or someone to go to if I have questions or concerns that I know will take me seriously?

_____

_____

_____

_____

_____

Now, some of these questions, depending on your answers, require follow-up. And you're smart enough to know which ones— there are resources available to you if there are things you need or want to work on that have seemingly little to do with a relationship, but your feelings about yourself absolutely affect your relationships. There is a list of resources at the end of this book, and you should also have available to you a school counselor, psychologist, or family doctor who could help with some of these things. Please reach out if you need to.

RE-DRAWING THE LINE

"You're so whipped."

— TEENAGE GUYS EVERYWHERE FROM, LIKE, 1995+

Sigh. I guess I get it. But this phrase is so overused to where anytime a guy does something genuinely nice for his significant other, he's "whipped." It's part of the whole "be a man" culture that any type of sensitivity is frowned upon, and I feel like we should be over it. Now, as a side note, if someone is being emotionally controlled or manipulated by a significant other, that is absolutely a problem and I get the negativity. In that instance, "whipped" seems too light of a term. Overall, I just don't like it.

———

The thing is, lines can be moved and re-drawn when needed. Because again, human complexity is a tricky business. People grow and evolve, and they change their minds. So the "drawing the line" conversation isn't a one-time deal. Boundaries should be revisited often, especially in a long-term relationship or one that is on-and-off. And just because you (or a partner) agreed to something once, doesn't mean it's a given. That's the thing about consent—it's an every-single-time thing. This does not mean you must have an hour-long conversation every time you want to hook up, but there should absolutely be a moment of "you good?" asked with sincerity.

Sometimes re-drawing the line is even more difficult than that first conversation because maybe you'd found yourself in a routine. But you owe yourself one maybe-uncomfortable conversation every once in a while if it means you're making sure things work for you.

<3 Nicole

BI-BI-BI

It was one hundred and fifteen percent too early to be conscious, but if I was late, I had zero chance of staying on my coach's good side, meaning zero chance of being captain of my team in the fall.

"Fine," I groaned aloud to no one. I found the nearest pair of volleyball shorts on my floor and one clean Gem City shirt hanging in my closet, so it was a win so far. The fact that my mom had set the coffee maker last night and there was an incredibly sexy pot of coffee waiting for me when I got downstairs was a bonus. My shoes would eventually be tied, but that they were on my feet was good enough, and I shuffled out to my car.

I backed out and pushed the button on my dash for Blue-tooth, and the eight billion decibels of Rage Against the Machine woke me right the hell up. "Shit!" I yelled silently, turning down the stereo. My heart was pounding, but I assumed that was better than potentially falling asleep at the wheel. *Looking like an awesome day.*

I loved volleyball. I also loved sleep, but apparently, volley-ball won, as evidenced by my jogging into the gym of a high school three towns away from my own.

I spotted a few of my teammates across the gym and headed that way. *At least I'm in the right place.*

"Carly?" I heard from my left.

I turned to find a very familiar looking brunette dressed in blue and gold.

"Sara?" I asked, slightly taken aback, while she skipped up to me, her short brown hair bouncing along with her. She threw her arms around my neck, almost knocking me over.

"Oh my god! It's been like sixty years!" I felt warmth spread from my chest to my cheeks when my arms closed around her back, wondering if I remembered the last time we saw each other accurately.

"Yeah..." I got out, pulling back and really looking at her. She was as cute as she'd always been— heart shaped face and green eyes and lips to die for.

She reached out and grabbed my hands, making my stomach do flips. "Listen, I gotta go and stretch, but when we break for lunch, we are catching up, okay?"

"Sure, that sounds good," I responded, remembering how to speak in sentences. She squeezed my hands and skipped back off to her team nearby. *What the hell just happened?* I shook my head and continued to walk to my team in a daze. The last time I'd hung out with Sara was three years ago at the end of eighth grade, just before she moved to Colorado. *Apparently she's moved back.*

"Hey, girl," my friend Amber said as I walked up to where some of my teammates were sitting. "You ready for all of this fun and conditioning today?" She feigned cheerfulness.

"If I still have all of my limbs tomorrow, I'll call it a victory," I responded. She pulled me back into the reason we were here—last camp before school started. I needed to focus, and my little blast from the past would have to wait until later. The feedback from a nearby megaphone let us know it was time to do awkward get-to-know-you games before the work started. There were members from at least eight schools there, but I saw some familiar faces anyway from playing club and doing a zillion camps before. No matter how hard I tried not to, my eyes searched for Sara, and I caught my breath when I found her looking at me. She shot me smile and then turned back to her friend.

"All right, ladies. Here is how the game is played— find someone you don't know, and discover three things you have in common. If you can do this before the whistle, find someone else and do the same. Ready... set... go!" The whistle blew and there was a slight shuffle of people moving, but honestly, no one is that excited for icebreakers. I felt a tap on my shoulder and turned to find Sara. Again.

"Do you think it counts if we haven't seen each other in a long time?"

"Well, I mean, if it's been six decades, I think we get a pass."

"Totally agree." Her smile hit me right in the gut, and part of me wished she wasn't there. "So. Three things in common. Are you still obsessed with Dr. Pepper?"

I laughed at that. I had had kind of an addiction back then. I straightened my blond ponytail and shook my head. "Nah. Mostly water and coffee for me now."

"Coffee! There's our first thing. I wouldn't survive without it."

"Same." I felt the corners of my mouth turn up. It didn't feel like any time had passed at all. "Do you still have five drawers of flannel pajamas?" This was a girl who had a different pair for every sleepover and every pajama day in elementary school.

"Don't judge me. They're very soft. I take it you're still a T-shirt and shorts girl?"

"If that," I found myself saying flirtatiously. I didn't know why. I didn't want to revisit rejection, but she was impossible not to flirt with.

"Well, not something in common, then, but making me think a sleepover is in order." *I'm sorry, what?*

"I think if we agree on that, it counts as something in common."

"Then two down," she stated, holding my gaze for so long I started to wonder if either of us would ever blink. "Do you have any plans this weekend?" I wasn't sure if this was still part of the game or not, or if she was asking me out...

"Um, not particularly. Hanging out with some friends, maybe going to the river."

Her smile faltered. "Cool," she replied awkwardly, totally losing her flirty vibe. *Okay, then.* "Maybe—"

Just then, the whistle blew, and we were ordered back to our teams. "I guess we can find the third thing at lunch," I offered.

"Yeah, definitely," Sara said, still seeming distracted as we parted ways.

Whatever. I'm not here to dredge up four-year-old crushes anyway. I walked back to my team and tried to forget it.

———

If I heard someone say, "Just one more set," again, it was probable that I would be arrested, at least for attempted murder. I had done more push-ups, more wind-sprints, and more burpees than could be deemed healthy. My clothes were now so sweaty they were just a part of me, and my ponytail had given up two hours ago. *Why do I do these things to myself?*

At least the torture allowed me to focus on something other than Sara and the memory of a night that was too long ago for it to get to me as much as it was. We'd both found ourselves with our own teams at lunch, and other than a wave across the gym, there was no catching up. I snuck a few glances, maybe, but it was probably for the best that we didn't try to make a thing of it. Sometimes friendships ended because they were supposed to.

"Are you going to the river tonight?" Amber asked between gulps of water.

"I don't know that I'll even make it to my bed when I get home, let alone to the river."

"Aw, I didn't take you for a quitter, Briggs."

"Then you absolutely have the wrong impression of me," I grinned, shaking my head.

"Jared will be there." She wiggled her eyebrows.

"Oh. Well, then I'll totally be there."

"Really?"

"No. Jared and I haven't been a thing for months."

"Oh! I'm sorry, I didn't—"

"Girl. Not a big deal. He's a drama king, and my heart was not broken. I hope it's an epic party though."

"Same," she grinned. "Text me if you change your mind."

"Yeah, yeah." I waved her off and shoved my now-empty water bottle into my bag and heaved myself to a standing position, wishing I was home and showered and in my bed. I saw Sara coming toward me, looking far too full of energy.

"You kind of kicked ass in that last scrimmage," she said as she got closer. Her clothes looked dry, and I vowed to research how to become one of those people who doesn't sweat profusely. It had to be witchcraft.

"Thanks. I think I'll regret that last dive later on, but all of me hurts right now, so who knows."

"I hear you. I was gonna go grab a slush from Sonic. And maybe an order or two of cheese tots. And a burger. And maybe a dessert. You in?"

"I literally look, and probably smell, like I crawled out of a sewer."

"You look hot. I'll drive and drop you back at your car." She turned on her heel and made for the exit without a second glance. *Okay, then. A little bossy, but that's sort of your type,* I thought to myself. I flung my bag over my shoulder and followed my past out into the parking lot.

She drove a little Miada, and I had to laugh. She used to insist that she would have a car just like Barbie's when we were kids, and she kind of did.

"I'm guessing this was a gift from your dad?" I asked.

"My mom was livid." She laughed, dropping into the driver's seat. Her dad never could say no.

"Well, at least it's a convertible and I can air out."

"Carly," she said, narrowing her eyes at me. "You look like you just kicked some serious ass. You're fierce. So shut up." She dropped a pair of sunglasses on her face to combat the late afternoon sun, and I resigned myself to the fact that it was going to be a really interesting ride.

————

It took a whole three minutes to get to Sonic, which was enough time for us to run out of small talk- school, where we were hoping to go to college, volleyball. I really wasn't good at chit-chat.

"So. Do you have a boyfriend?" I asked her after she'd parked in a shady spot and we got our food. I just needed to get it out of the way and figure out what the hell we were doing here. If this was really a friendly reunion or if the energy she was giving off was for real.

"No. No boyfriend." She shrugged, giving very little away.

"Girlfriend?" I asked, taking a brain-freeze-inducing drink of my slush and making it clear that I needed more information.

"Not at the moment." Her face was serious, and she met my gaze head on. *Plot twist.*

"Some things have changed then, in the past three years." I flashed back to our last sleepover, where I'd told Sara I thought I was bi. I realized I had more-than-friendly feelings for her in the sixth or seventh grade, but she was getting ready to move away, and I didn't know that I could let her leave without telling her *something*. I'd reached for her hand back then, like she was reaching for my hand now. The difference being that I let her take it in our present moment, and she had pulled away and told me she needed to get home. That was the last real conversation we'd ever had.

"They have. Listen, I'm really sorry about how we left things before I went to Colorado, Car. I was... I don't know. Scared, maybe?" No one had called me Car in a long time. Her hands were tiny like the rest of her, and she carefully wove her fingers with mine across our cheese tots. It was all very romantic.

"Yeah. So was I. Because I hadn't told anyone I was bi before." I pulled my hand back slightly, realizing I might just have some lingering resentment towards my old friend. "You were my best friend, and you just left."

"I know. I thought about you all the time, though. I couldn't believe it when you walked in the gym today. I felt like... maybe I could make things up to you." I didn't know what to do with the sincerity in her voice, paired with the tingles running up my arm and the memory of rejection in my head. Her fingers traced lines on my open palm, and I didn't pull back again. It was so surreal that she was sitting in front of me and there wasn't the barrier of fear she'd constructed in the past.

"Make it up to me, huh?" I asked, letting a smile play across my lips. Her eyes widened slightly at that, and she leaned in hesitantly. Her lips were full and perfect, and I thought my heart might leap out of my chest when they finally met mine. I felt her fingernails at my neck, and a shiver ran down my spine as her kiss deepened. *No way this is even happening right now*. I was pretty sure I'd be pissed off when I woke up.

Her skin was so soft, and I let my hands linger under her shirt. Her fingers traveled from my neck down my chest to in-between my legs.

"Hey," I said gently, placing my hand on her wrist.

"Hey," she said back. "What's wrong?"

"Nothing. We just need to take a step back."

"Oh. I'm sorry. You've been out for a long time... I just assumed you'd..." Her voice trailed off uncomfortably.

"Assumed I'd hook up with someone who's basically a stranger?" I tried to leave my voice neutral, but I was annoyed.

"No! Wait, I'm not a stranger." She looked confused.

"Sara... you're like... freaking gorgeous, and I'm definitely down to go out and I don't know, reconnect. That kiss was hot, but I don't really do random hookups. I'm not judging, if that's what you're into. That's just not me. When I hook up, especially with a girl... it's intense. I can't just do that and walk away."

"Okay...are you looking for something serious?" She said the word 'serious' like it might jump out and bite her.

"No? I don't know. I'm good with casual, but I'd like to actually figure out who you are first. At least, who you are now."

"I get that." She relaxed visibly. "Well, I am a girl who is going to finish all of this food alone if you don't start eating."

"I would fight you for the food." I laughed, feeling more at ease. It felt like a piece of our friendship had definitely survived.

"Okay, if I share the tots, can I kiss you again?"

"How could I turn down a solid gold offer like that?" I leaned in and kissed her first, and I started to actually believe this might be real.

What do you think of the way Carly handled herself with her old friend?

_____

_____

_____

_____

_____

How do you feel about giving second chances in your own life? Do you think Carly was right to do so here?

_____

_____

_____

_____

_____

In what way did Carly "re-draw" the line with Sara?

_____

_____

_____

_____

_____

Do you think Sara felt rejected? How did she deal with Carly telling her to stop?

_____

_____

_____

_____

_____

What can you take away from this story?

_____

_____

_____

_____

_____

YOUR TURN: PERSONAL JOURNAL
REVISITING DECISIONS

You know what they say about assume, right? If not, Google that one ;). But really, just because you make a decision doesn't mean it's forever. If it did, we'd all be firemen or famous singers and stay with our high school sweethearts forever and ever.

Bottom line: You are in control of your path. If you're not happy, you can choose to make a decision to change it and accept that it might be painful. You can accept that you might cause someone else pain, knowing that in the long run, it's for the best. These are not easy decisions that can be made with a pro-con list. These are decisions that require you to look into yourself and into your future and take a leap of faith that you're doing the right thing (side note: no one ever really knows for sure if they're making the right choice— we all just cross our fingers and do what we think is best).

This part of the journal may not be relevant at this moment. It might be a year from now that you realize you're stuck or unhappy or ready for a change, and I hope you'll come back to this page and do the work that needs to be done. Good for you for recognizing what works and what doesn't and being brave enough to want to change it.

Feeling	Cause	Possible Change	Consequence/Effect of that Change	Can I handle it?

Brain Emptying Activity:

It may sound like a bad thing to empty your brain, but really, once all of your thoughts and worries are on paper, it's easier to sort through them, prioritize them, and let them go. So go ahead, everything that's going through your mind, put it here. Then think about highlighting the really important stuff and starting there. Chances are, all the little things are related to that anyway.

WHAT ABOUT ME?

Men want "a lady in the streets but a freak in the bed."

—Ludacris

Sorry not sorry, I'm not on board. Want what you want, be clear about it, and don't buy into this stereotype that all men want one thing or that all women need to be one thing. You do you.

———

This might be the most important section of this book. Because I can tell you that no matter how well you know yourself or how many conversations you've had, you cannot control everything that happens to you. And in those situations, you must take care of yourself. Whether that means walking away, asking for help, reporting a crime, talking to your friends and family, seeing a therapist or a medical professional, a school counselor, calling a hotline— whatever you need to do to take care of yourself, you do that and don't apologize for it.

If you find yourself in need of help, please view the resources in the back of this book, speak to someone you trust, and know that you're not alone.

Just because this is the end of the book, doesn't mean it's the end of the conversation. This culture we live in won't get better until these conversations become the norm. So common that you couldn't imagine not having them. So keep talking, and take care of yourself

Trigger warning: Angel and My Demons references sexual assault.

<3 Nicole

ANGEL AND MY DEMONS
** TRIGGER WARNING: MENTION OF SEXUAL
ASSAULT/RAPE **

I'd come home from college for the weekend feeling like a
rock star. And now I wanted to crawl in a hole. I stayed in
my room for most of Saturday if I didn't count the three
showers, only coming out when my mom threatened to
move my ass back home if I didn't socialize with the family
when I was visiting.

I just kept replaying it over and over in my head, and I
couldn't for the life of me figure out why I didn't just *say*
something. I wasn't a particularly quiet girl on a normal
day, but in that moment, I had nothing to say? My head
pounded when I thought about it.

Shea: Em, why have you gone AWOL? Are you embarrassed or something? Because I've done way sluttier things
with less hot guys. You know you don't need to freak out.

Me: I don't know.

. . .

That was the most honest statement I could make.

Shea: Well, stop it, and come out with me tonight.

Me: I'm not in a mood to go out. Maybe breakfast tomorrow or something.

Shea: Lammmmmmmmmme. Fine, whatever, but you better ask me about Brian at breakfast.

Me: Will do. Promise.

I hoped I could bounce back from this by then. I kept opening Angel's text and wishing I could just rewind and leave with him from that stupid party. After looking at it for the hundredth time, I decided I just had to fix it. I didn't know how, but I couldn't go back to school without trying. Even if we weren't... well, anything, we'd been friends a long time, and it killed me that I might have ruined that.

I threw on a hoodie and a pair of jeans and got in my hatch-back. I knew if I texted or called him, he could just hang up, but he'd talk to me in person. I had zero idea what I was going to say, and I just prayed that the knot in my throat wouldn't give way to tears.

———

I pulled up outside his ranch-style house and realized he might not even be home. *This was stupid.* I just didn't know what else to do. I got out and swung my door shut, shoving my hands into my hoodie pockets despite the 90-degree weather. *One foot in front of the other.*

I made it to the front door and rang the bell, sighing with relief or disappointment when one of his little sisters answered.

"Hi, is Angel home?"

"Yeah, hang on," she replied, running back into the house. A few seconds later, he emerged, a confused look on his face when he saw me.

"What?" he asked plainly.

"I, um, I just needed to talk to you." I smoothed down my hair, wishing I'd bothered to look in a mirror at some point.

"Why don't you go talk to Jake?" His expression showed hurt rather than anger, but it felt the same to me. That knot in my throat that I'd hoped would chill? It grew spikes— I couldn't breathe. I tried to suck in air and answer him, but instead I dropped to the ground and hugged my knees. I just needed to calm down. Angel's face had changed when I looked back up at him.

"Em. *Dime*. Please." He bent down next to me and spoke softly, which only made me cry harder.

"I don't know what happened, and I don't know what to do," I got out.

"What do you mean you don't know what happened?" He was sitting in front of me now on his front porch.

"I just... I woke up and he was there. And I didn't say anything. I didn't do anything. I don't know why, I mean, you know me. I didn't even talk to him." It came out as a jumbled-up mess.

He was quiet for longer than was comfortable. "Are you saying that Jake raped you?" Angel asked, his jaw clenched.

"No! I mean, that's… that's not something he would do. Right?" The word rape sounded so Law and Order, and I couldn't wrap my head around it. *It was just a stupid party thing.*

"Em," Angel began, letting his fingers rest on my arms, "did you say yes?"

"No… I mean, I didn't really say anything."

"*Chingada madre.*" I didn't know what that meant, but it didn't sound good.

"I'm sorry… I really wanted to go out with you, and I should've just left when you—"

"Stop. I'm sorry. Really sorry. I didn't ask, I just… I was dick. I'm sorry."

I hugged my knees, feeling a rush of relief at the fact that he believed me, but there was still the pit in the bottom of my stomach about what he'd said. "Do you really think that? That he, like… I don't know."

"I don't think it matters what I think."

"I just should've left with you. I should've said something else."

"Em…"

"Yeah?"

"I'm gonna kill him." The look in his eyes was resigned, like he actually had no choice but to commit murder."

"I'd rather you stayed out of jail."

"What do you need from me?"

"I just don't want you to hate me."

"*Nunca.* Never."

I rubbed my eyes with the sleeves of my sweatshirt, sweating now, sitting on the concrete in the sun. "Okay. Then I think we're good. I just couldn't take thinking about you hating me and thinking that I..."

"Will you come in? Hang out for a bit."

I wanted someone to just tell me that everything was fine, that I'd feel better tomorrow when I realized this wasn't that big of a deal. And Angel wasn't doing that. My heart was beating harder the more I thought about the implications of last night. "I, um, I think I might just go home? I feel... I don't know. I feel weird."

"I think when you get back to school? You should talk to someone, yeah?"

"Yeah. Maybe."

"And Em?"

"Yeah."

"I could never hate you. I thought... well, I was jealous. I didn't hate you. And now I feel like a complete asshole for even feeling that way."

"You're not. You're... well, you're the opposite of that."

"If I can't get you to come in, will you text me later?"

"Sure."

"I mean it, though. Like take care of yourself, and if I can do something... murder, just your average assault, something, tell me. Okay?"

I managed a laugh. "Okay. I'll let you know if there are any crimes I need you to commit on my behalf."

"Good." He held out his hands and pulled me up to standing, and he let his fingers linger between mine. "Next time you're home... we're going out. Even if it's just as friends."

"That sounds good. Thanks."

He stepped in and pecked my cheek lightly, and I made my way back to my car, sweat dripping down my back. When I'd come over, I felt like the roar in my head was too loud to think, to focus. Now, it was too quiet, and I had too much to think about. I'd always thought of rape as something that happened on TV and in an alley somewhere. Not on my friend's couch. *This is so fucked up.*

I didn't know exactly what to do, but I thought I'd take Angel's suggestion and see a counselor on campus when I got back. Someone who didn't know me, who didn't know Jake, and could maybe make some sense of the slime coating my skin every time I thought about it. But having Angel look at me like he understood what I was saying made me feel like I wasn't so crazy, and that was going to have to be good enough for a step one.

Why do you think Emma hasn't reached out to her parents or gone to the police at this point? What is her motivation for making the decisions she has made so far?

_____

_____

_____

_____

_____

How do you feel about Angel's response after he talks to Emma in person?

_____

_____

_____

_____

_____

What role does reputation play in a story like this? Should it have a role at all?

_____

_____

_____

_____

_____

Do you think Emma's reputation (or any else's) would be affected if this became public?

_____

_____

_____

_____

_____

What does Emma need to do to take care of herself?

_____

_____

_____

_____

_____

What can you take away from this story?

_____

_____

_____

_____

_____

Thoughts:

_____

_____

_____

_____

_____

_____

_____

_____

_____

_____

_____

_____

_____

_____

_____

_____

_____

_____

_____

_____

_____

YOUR TURN: PERSONAL JOURNAL
TAKING CARE OF YOURSELF

This story hits hard, not because it's so unbelievable that this could happen, but because we all know someone it's happened to, or it's happened to us. It's brushed off as a "crazy party" or mentioned as "did you see how fucked up so-and-so was?"

None of it is okay. This book wasn't written to deal with sexual assault, because I, as a teacher and writer, do not have the skills nor the background to explain how to deal with that. I have experienced sexual assault, and I wish I'd had more resources to help me figure out how to deal, besides the "eh, it happens" approach. It does happen, but it shouldn't. No one has that right.

So, this section is about two things— figuring out what you need in a healthy relationship, and figuring out where to turn in the event that you're not. I hope the latter is never the case, but knowledge is power, and I want you to have that power.

. . .

Top Five Things you Need in a Healthy Relationship:

_____

_____

_____

_____

_____

#RelationshipGoals

Yes, you know the hashtag, but really it's not a bad idea to think about things you see in others' relationships that you would like to have in yours. Now, this can be a slippery slope between having a goal and comparing your relationship to someone else's, so I caution you that you don't ever _really_ know everything about someone else or someone else's relationship. So take away what you can from the positive while knowing that perfection doesn't exist.

Think about couples you know of that you admire, and why you admire them. This could be anything from TV or movie or book characters to your great-grandparents who have been married 60 years. Think about all the work you've done to narrow down what you see for yourself, and think of examples. It's totally fine if this section stays empty for a while. Now that you're thinking about it, you might see some things come up that you want to remember, so come and jot them down then.

#RelationshipGoals:

_____

_____

_____

_____

_____

_____

_____

_____

_____

_____

RESOURCES

Resources Specific to Sexual Assault/Rape

Resource	Website	Phone Number
RAINN	Rainn.org	800-656-HOPE
Mental Health America	Mentalhealthamerica.net	800-656-HOPE
Planned Parenthood	PlannedParenthood.org	800-230-7526
Colorado Coalition Against Sexual Assault	Ccasa.org/gethelp	303-839-9999
Law Enforcement		911
Mental Health Services	http://www.mentalhealthamerica.net/finding-therapy	

Resources Specific to Sex Education

TeenSource	Teensource.org	
Stay Teen	Stayteen.org/sex-ed	
Scarleteen	Scarleteen.com	

THANK YOU

Thank you for reading. I would love for you to leave a review for this journal on Amazon and to tell a friend (or 10). Having these conversations and doing this work is *so* important for every young adult, and I hope that this book makes it into all the right hands.

Thank you for putting in the time and effort to work on this journal. I'd love to hear from you on my website, Instagram, or Facebook page, so please do visit and let me know what you thought!

Website: NicoleCampbellBooks.com
Insta: NicoleCampbellBooks
FB: NicoleCampebellBooks

Lightning Source UK Ltd.
Milton Keynes UK
UKHW022036180121
377284UK00012B/1010/J

9 781034 245315